General editor: Graham Handley

Brodie's Notes on Charles Dickens's

Great Expectations

T. W. Smith BA
Former English Master, Barrow and Teignmouth Grammar Schools

M
MACMILLAN

© The Macmillan Press Ltd 1990

First edition published 1952 by James Brodie Ltd
First Pan edition published1976
This new edition published 1990
by Pan Books Ltd

Published 1993 by
MACMILLAN PRESS LTD
Houndmills, Basingstoke, Hampshire RG21 2XS
and London
Companies and representatives
throughout the world

ISBN 0–333–58072–9

Printed in Great Britain by
Cox and Wyman Ltd
Reading, Berkshire

Reprinted 1995

Contents

Preface

The intention throughout this study aid is to stimulate and guide, to encourage your involvement in the book, and to develop informed responses and a sure understanding of the main details.

Brodie's Notes provide a clear outline of the play or novel's plot, followed by act, scene, or chapter summaries and/or commentaries. These are designed to emphasize the most important literary and factual details. Poems, stories or non-fiction texts combine brief summary with critical commentary on individual aspects or common features of the genre being examined. Textual notes define what is difficult or obscure and emphasize literary qualities. Revision questions are set at appropriate points to test your ability to appreciate the prescribed book and to write accurately and relevantly about it.

In addition, each of these Notes includes a critical appreciation of the author's art. This covers such major elements as characterization, style, structure, setting and themes. Poems are examined technically – rhyme, rhythm, for instance. In fact, any important aspect of the prescribed work will be evaluated. The aim is to send you back to the text you are studying.

Each study aid concludes with a series of general questions which require a detailed knowledge of the book: some of these questions may invite comparison with other books, some will be suitable for coursework exercises, and some could be adapted to work you are doing on another book or books. Each study aid has been adapted to meet the needs of the current examination requirements. They provide a basic, individual and imaginative response to the work being studied, and it is hoped that they will stimulate you to acquire disciplined reading habits and critical fluency.

Graham Handley 1990

The author and his work

Charles John Huffham Dickens was born on 7 February 1812 at Portsea, the eldest son of John and Elizabeth Dickens. His father was a clerk in the Navy Pay Office at Portsmouth, and was in many respects the prototype of the thriftless but perennially optimistic Mr Micawber in *David Copperfield*, the earlier chapters of which are based on Dickens's childhood. In 1814 he was transferred to London and in 1816 to Chatham, where the elder Dickens once told his son that, if he persevered, he might one day come to live in Gad's Hill Place (near Rochester), a prophecy that was to be fulfilled. In 1823 the family moved to Camden Town, London, and shortly afterwards, because of his financial difficulties, Mr Dickens was sent to the Marshalsea (debtors') Prison. During this time the boy was employed in a blacking factory, where his sensitive nature suffered more from the humiliation than any actual ill-treatment.

When his father was retired on a pension, Dickens was given two years of regular education, then entered the office of a Gray's Inn solicitor, where in eighteen months he acquired a knowledge of the law that he used with much effect in *Great Expectations*. He worked hard at shorthand, and in 1835 joined the staff of the *Morning Chronicle*, on which his father had already found a post. He was a parliamentary and descriptive reporter for seventeen years, travelling round the country by coach – remarkable for his keenness of observation and imaginative powers.

As a boy Dickens had read eagerly the works of Smollett, Fielding, Cervantes and other classical novelists and as a young man he spent much time studying in the British Museum. In 1834 his first article was published; by 1836 his *Sketches by Boz* in the *Evening Chronicle* had drawn sufficient attention for him to publish them in two volumes. In the same year he married the daughter of the editor of the *Evening Chronicle*, Catherine Hogarth. He was next asked by Chapman and Hall to write the text to accompany a series of Cockney sporting plates, but a change of plan led to the formation of an imaginary club of sporting gentlemen, and *Pickwick Papers* began to appear in serial form in 1837. Their characteristic humour and pathos brought him instant fame. *Oliver Twist* and *Nicholas Nickleby* were soon being written simultaneously and other novels appeared at the rate of about one a year. Publication in monthly parts made great demands upon him and some of Dickens's work suffers from this pressure.

In 1842 Dickens went to America where he was given a great reception. The satire in the *American Notes* (1842) and the novel *Martin Chuzzlewit* (1843) which dwelt on his American experiences caused some offence over there for a time but his second visit, in 1867, was an even greater success. In 1856 he purchased Gad's Hill Place, the dream of his childhood. He immediately began a series of improvements, and did not reside there permanently till 1860 by which time he was separated from his wife. His eldest son, Charles, employed by a London tea-merchant, had gone out to Hong Kong to buy tea on his own account. Surrounded by the rest of his large family, Dickens enjoyed being 'squire' to the villagers and played an active part in games and social festivities, especially at Christmas.

When quite young, Dickens had been taken to the theatre by a relative to see Shakespeare's *Richard III*. This experience began a lifelong love of the stage. In those early days he used often to act as well as tell stories. In later years he was for a time the manager of an amateur theatrical company. His greatest stage performance, however, was the reading of extracts from his books to enthusiastic audiences here and in America, often for charity. The passages chosen were usually the most dramatic and therefore the most exhausting; the work affected his health and he was eventually compelled to give it up.

In 1859 he started a magazine of his own, *All the Year Round*, in which *Great Expectations* appeared (1861). It was written during an interval between two reading tours and the author spent many pleasant hours striding along the country lanes around his home. A favourite walk was one of some five miles to the lonely churchyard of Cooling on the edge of the marshes between the Thames and the Medway. He frequently strolled the streets of Rochester where, in the Vines, stands the original of Satis House. The end of the story is said to have been composed on board a steamer on an excursion from London to the mouth of the Thames in which he spent one night at a riverside inn, 'The Ship and Lobster'! The story originated in a paper intended as one of a series collected under the title of *The Uncommercial Traveller* (i.e. one interested not in business orders but the human scene).

In a letter published by John Forster in his biography Dickens wrote:

For a little piece I have been writing ... such a very fine, new and grotesque idea has opened upon me, that I begin to doubt whether I had not better cancel the little paper, and reserve the notion for a new book.

Later he added:

The book will be written in the first person throughout, and during these first three weekly numbers you will find the hero to be a boy-child, like David. Then he will be an apprentice ... I have made the opening, I hope, in its general effect exceedingly droll. I have put a child and a good-natured foolish man in relations that seem to me very funny.

Dickens's last work, *The Mystery of Edwin Drood*, was stopped in 1870 by his death, from a stroke, in his home. After his burial in Westminster Abbey crowds filed reverently past his grave. His wide human sympathies, his spirited attacks on social evils, his vivid characterization and the entertainment he gave his readers, made him the best-loved novelist of the century.

Childhood Memories

The reader will find in the second chapter of Forster's Life a moving account of the boy's time at Robert Warren's blacking warehouse in the Strand, later moved to Chandos Street, Covent Garden. The pleasant enough life at Chatham (from Dickens's fifth to his ninth year) had been replaced by a lonely existence of wandering along London streets; as a substitute for non-existent boy companions there were some works of fiction in his father's house, though indeed some of these in family crises were to be lost to the pawn shop. These early experiences remained a 'secret', not referred to by Charles or his parents, and revealed only to a few kindred spirits like his biographer or transmuted into episodes in certain novels.

Looking back, rather like the older Pip, on his daily occupation of tying up and labelling pots of blacking, he wrote:

I know that I worked, from morning to night, with common men and boys, a shabby child ... I soon became at least as expeditious and as skilful with my hands, as either of the other boys. Though perfectly familiar with them, my conduct and manners were different enough from theirs to place a space between us. They, and the men, always spoke of me as 'the young gentleman' ... No advice, no counsel, no encouragement, no consolation, no support, from anyone that I can call to mind.

Dickens himself avoided going anywhere near the scenes of his youthful humiliation; curiously he makes Joe on his visit to Pip in London go specially to see a fictional 'Blacking Ware'us' and criticize its ostentatious architecture (Chapter 27).

Mr Wopsle dying 'exceedingly game on Bosworth Field' was probably promoted by recollection of a performance in Chatham of Shakespeare's play when Dickens was:

at any rate old enough to recollect how his young heart leapt with terror as the wicked King Richard, struggling for life against the virtuous Richmond, backed up and bumped against the box in which he was. (Forster, Ch. I).

The education offered by Mr Wopsle's great-aunt seems a shade less extraordinary when we read accounts, by Dickens and other former pupils, of the Wellington House Academy in the Hampstead Road, attended by Dickens from twelve to fourteen years of age.

It was considered at the time a very superior sort of school ... but it was most shamefully mismanaged, and the boys made but very little progress. The proprietor, Mr Jones, was a Welshman; a most ignorant fellow, and a mere tyrant, whose chief employment was to scourge the boys.

Dickens himself describes it as:

remarkable for white mice ... the boys trained the mice much better than the master trained the boys.

Plot

As is often the case in Dickens's novels, *Great Expectations* has a very involved plot. The reader is presented with the results long before the causes which may come as complete surprises and there is usually much mystification. In the following outline the events of the story have been re-arranged in chronological order.

A wealthy brewer named Havisham, living at Satis House in a market town not far from the south bank of the Thames Estuary, had a daughter by his first wife and a son by his second. The son, Arthur, was a wastrel who, jealous that his half-sister had been left much more of his father's wealth than he had, leagued himself with a good-looking, well-educated intriguer called Compeyson. The latter won Miss Havisham's affections to such an extent that she followed his advice implicitly and disregarded that of her relations. When Compeyson swindled her of large sums of money and finally persuaded her to buy Arthur's share in the brewery for an exorbitant amount, her cousin, Matthew Pocket, warned her against him and was ordered out of the house for good. Miss Havisham was to have been married to Compeyson but he brutally broke it off by letter on the wedding morning and the wicked pair, after spending the money thus obtained, took to a criminal life.

Arthur died in delirium, imagining his sister was putting a shroud on him; Compeyson had meanwhile enlisted Abel Magwitch to help him with forgeries. Magwitch had been in and out of prison from youth and at that time had a baby daughter by a gipsy woman, Molly, who had recently been charged with the murder of another woman of whom she was jealous. The case for the defence was the first important one undertaken by a lawyer, Jaggers, who succeeded in getting her acquitted but Magwitch had gone into hiding at the time of the trial. Compeyson knew this and used it as a hold over him. Both were eventually arrested for circulating stolen bank notes but in court Compeyson's counsel managed to put most of the blame on to Magwitch so that the latter's sentence was twice as heavy.

When both escaped from the Hulks on the Thames in which

they were serving their sentences, Magwitch, intent on revenge, forfeited his chance of getting away by hunting down Compeyson on the marshes north of the town in which Miss Havisham lived. The result was that they were re-taken struggling together in a ditch and Magwitch now received a life-sentence and was transported to Australia. During his brief spell of liberty Magwitch had surprised a boy in a village churchyard on the edge of the marshes. He frightened him into stealing a file and some food from his home, where he lived, an orphan, with his harsh sister and her husband, Joe Gargery, the village blacksmith. This the boy did without betraying him and thus enabled him to file away one of his leg-irons. Magwitch remembered this with gratitude, especially as the boy was about the same age as his little girl, whom he believed to have been murdered by her wild mother.

Actually the mother had been taken permanently into his service by Jaggers immediately after the trial; when the lawyer was told by Miss Havisham that she wanted to adopt a little girl he took Magwitch's child, Estella, to Satis House, now a darkened, decaying household. Broken hearted by her deceiver's letter, Miss Havisham had ordered everything, including the wedding feast, to remain as it was, stopped all the clocks and closed out the sunlight. She lived as a recluse, still wearing her bridal dress, and proceeded to rear the girl with the intention that she should avenge her patroness by breaking a man's heart when she grew up. One day, in pursuance of her grim purpose, she asked a tenant of hers, Pumblechook, for a boy to go and 'play' at her house. Pumblechook, a frequent visitor to the blacksmith's in the village by the marshes and 'uncle' to the boy, at once thought of him and brought the news to Mrs Gargery, who saw in the invitation an opportunity for the boy to make his way in life and be off her hands.

Thus it was that Pip (short for Philip Pirrip), the hero of the novel, came on that 'memorable day' to Satis where he was mercilessly teased by Estella and made to feel ashamed of his commonness. Pip was frequently employed for hours at a stretch, wheeling Miss Havisham round the two rooms in which she lived and eventually for this she gave Joe Gargery twenty-five guineas to pay for Pip's apprenticeship to the blacksmith's trade. The visits ceased; not until a year later did Pip call at the big house, ostensibly to thank Miss Havisham, but in reality to see Estella with whom the boy was hopelessly in love. Miss

Havisham was there as usual but Estella had gone to a finishing school in France and the boy came away more dissatisfied than ever with the humbleness of his own home surroundings. When he got back he found his sister had been murderously attacked (by Orlick, Joe's assistant, with the convict's leg-iron picked up on the marshes); she remained a permanent invalid till her death and Biddy, a true-hearted village girl who first helped Pip to learn his letters, came to the forge to take charge.

Three years later Jaggers was commissioned by Magwitch, who had made a fortune by sheep-rearing in New South Wales, to give the blacksmith's boy the education of a gentleman, to fit him to inherit his wealth. The name of Pip's benefactor was to be kept a secret till he chose to reveal it himself in person and Pip assumed that the anonymous author of his 'Great Expectations' was Miss Havisham and that Estella was also destined to be his. He went to London, where he studied under Matthew Pocket at Hammersmith and lived in rooms in town with Herbert, Pocket's son, whom he had first met as a boy and with whom he had had a fight at Satis House. Herbert was now employed in an office with very poor prospects. The two young men became friends for life and, among other things, took up rowing on the Thames. Pip also formed a close acquaintance with Wemmick, Jaggers's clerk, who, out of office hours, was to prove of the greatest assistance to him.

One day Joe came up to London with a message from Miss Havisham that Estella had returned to Satis and would be glad to see Pip. His youthful love for the intended breaker of his heart was now intensified by her beauty as a young woman but she warned him that all tenderness had been bred out of her by Miss Havisham. Before long she came to reside with a family at Richmond who were to introduce her to society and Pip was required to accompany her on social engagements, a duty which proved more of a torture than a pleasure. Since his change of fortune Pip had shamefacedly avoided his humble relations at the forge and his remorse for neglecting Joe, the devotedly faithful companion of his childhood, was deepened after he (Pip) had been suddenly called home to the funeral of his sister. The shallowness of his promise to go back more often was unmasked by the shrewd but tactful Biddy. Back in London Pip gained some happiness by secretly negotiating a partnership for Herbert with some of his money but was dismayed to find Estella encouraging the advances of a boorish fellow called Drummle whom he had first met studying under Matthew Pocket (who largely depended for his livelihood on private tutoring). He found little consolation in Estella's generous confession that she wanted to spare Pip, alone of all men, the unhappiness of becoming her victim.

When Pip was twenty-three the blow fell which shattered all his dreams. Magwitch, who had returned from Australia at the risk of his life in order to see the young 'gentleman' he had created, made himself known to Pip in his rooms at the Temple. He had assumed the name of 'Provis' and Pip decided to call him his uncle. Unknown to them, the ex-convict's movements had already been spied by Orlick who hated Pip for getting him discharged by Miss Havisham from his employment at Satis as porter. He had gone there after leaving the forge where he had been making himself a nuisance by his attentions to Biddy. Pip and Herbert decided that Magwitch must be taken abroad again and, if necessary, that Pip should accompany him. Before any further steps were taken Pip visited Satis and learnt that Estella was to be married to Drummle – in order to spare him. On his return to London a note from Wemmick warned him not to go to his rooms; next day he saw the clerk at his house in the suburbs and was told he was being watched. 'Provis' was immediately taken down river to stay in the same house as Herbert's fiancée, Clara Barley, and Pip and Herbert started rowing regularly in preparation for the day when they might row from Magwitch's hide-out to an outward steamer for Pip and his benefactor to get on board and out of the country.

Some weeks passed in this way when Pip was once more summoned by Miss Havisham. She first gave him a cheque for nine hundred pounds after his earlier appeal for assistance (which he himself could no longer give, having made up his mind not to touch Magwitch's money) in completing the partnership for Herbert; and then she asked his forgiveness for the hard-hearted trick she had played on his affections. He was about to leave after a last tour of the grounds in which he had once walked with Estella when recurrence of a boyhood vision of Miss Havisham hanging from a beam prompted him to return upstairs in time to see her clothes catch light and to smother the flames, suffering burns himself.

Leaving her unconscious in the care of a surgeon and giving

instructions that Estella should be sent for, Pip returned to London, where his arm was dressed by Herbert. His friend was soon full of business prospects because the cheque enabled a new branch to be opened in the East where Herbert was to go and take charge. Then a note from Wemmick warned them to get Magwitch away in two days' time. The same day an anonymous missive referring to his 'Uncle Provis' enticed Pip to a lonely part of the marshes where he narrowly escaped being murdered by Orlick; Herbert, having found the note and followed him, arrived just in time. After a day's rest they rowed down river with another friend, picked up Magwitch and spent the night at a lonely riverside inn, where they heard of a mysterious boat hovering in the neighbourhood.

Next morning they were about to board a Hamburg steamer when the other boat appeared and they were called on board by officers (who had a heavily muffled informer with them) and asked to surrender Magwitch as a returned convict. The police boat had drawn alongside just as the steamer was bearing down upon them, and at the moment of impact Pip's boat was run down as Magwitch seized and unmasked the informer, who proved to be Compeyson. Pip and his friends were rescued but the two ex-convicts disappeared, struggling. Compeyson did not come to the surface again while Magwitch was picked up and taken to prison where, as a result of his injuries from the paddle-steamer, he was placed in the infirmary and regularly visited by Pip, who was devoted to his benefactor now that he had nothing to expect from him. In the interval before the trial he saw Wemmick happily married. At the next Sessions Magwitch was duly condemned to death but he died before the date of the execution, not, however, before Pip told him that his daughter had grown into a beautiful woman and that he himself was in love with her.

The strain of events brought on a fever from which Pip recovered after some weeks. He found by his bedside Joe Gargery, his faithful but neglected friend, who had nursed him through his illness. When Pip was restored to health Joe tactfully left for home early one morning, leaving a note and a receipt for a debt Pip had incurred and was unable to settle. Three days later Pip followed, having made up his mind to live at the forge and to ask Biddy to overlook the past and marry him. He arrived to find Biddy just married to Joe. After a farewell to his oldest friends and the familiar surroundings of his youth, he accepted Herbert's offer of a clerkship in the office in the East.

Eleven years later, now a partner, Pip returned to England and found Joe and Biddy happy with their growing family. Visiting the site of Satis House which had been pulled down he encountered Estella, also paying it a last farewell. She had been ill-treated by Drummle, before separating from him, but was now freed by his death. Her heart had been changed by her sufferings and she asked Pip's forgiveness. Together they left the ruins of the strange house in which they had first met 'never to part again'.

Chapter summaries, commentaries, textual notes and revision questions

Chapter 1

'Pip' begins the story of his rather disappointing life in a neglected churchyard in the desolate landscape of marshland in north Kent. The young orphan's reflections on the graves of his parents and five older brothers are suddenly interrupted by the frightening figure of a fugitive from the convict hulks off-shore in the Thames estuary. The latter first terrifies him and then elicits a promise by the boy to bring him early next morning from his home some food and a file (to free one leg from its iron fetter).

This opening chapter is probably the best-remembered episode in the novel. The grim picture of the flat desolate countryside, drawn in horizontal lines and relieved only by the forbidding vertical outlines of a beacon and a gibbet, is brought to life in the most brutal fashion by the most unlikely originator at a future date of Pip's 'great expectations'. On his early induction by a criminal to a criminal act rests the whole structure of this tale of deception and delusion – but also of lasting devotion.

In Dickens's later novels his curious blend of close observation of the comic in human life with remarkable analogies that grew in fantasy and exaggeration is already evident here: Pip's upside-down view of the church steeple, the hungry convict's incipient cannibalism and the unconvincing young man who tears out a boy's heart and liver. More effective are 'the cattle lifting their heads to look after him'.

the marsh country Part of the peninsula, some ten miles across, between the estuaries of the Thames and the Medway.
the flat in-shore Level ground at some distance from the sea.
pollards Trees of which the branches have been cut back to a certain height.
wittles Slang for 'victuals'.
Battery Gun emplacement.
'Much of that' i.e. not a good night.

Chapter 2

On his return home Pip learns from the blacksmith, Joe Gargery, that his wife, Pip's sister, who is twenty years older and his only surviving relative, has been out looking for him, carrying a cane with which to punish him. Mrs Joe is soon back and pounces on her small brother hiding behind the door. After some ferocious treatment she upbraids Pip for his ingratitude to the sister who saved him from the churchyard and brought him up 'by hand' – a method which, though earning her a reputation locally, has little sisterly affection. Her harsh character, symbolized by the permanent apron stuck with pins and needles, finds expression in her two main grudges: having to 'mother' Pip and being married to a blacksmith.

Forgetting that it is Christmas Eve with more food in the larder than usual Pip goes through the unnecessary agony of hiding, instead of eating, his half of the evening slice of bread and butter, with the result that Joe betrays his act of 'bolting' his food and Pip is dosed with tar-water. Hearing a gun Pip is so curious to know its significance that after being told that a second prisoner must have escaped from the Hulks, he is warned by Mrs Joe that criminal careers begin with asking questions. Waiting through a sleepless night until the dawn breaks Pip raids the pantry for food and drink and Joe's forge for a file and then sets off for the marshes.

The interior and the atmosphere of Pip's home, grimmer perhaps than the very marshes so close at hand, are vividly portrayed. Mrs Joe's sarcasm proves as heavy-handed as her physical treatment of her two charges; somewhat contradictory is her intense worry over the absence of Pip and her declared regret at having preserved his life. Already the reader's sympathy has been aroused for the youthful hero, tormented equally by his fears and his conscience.

also in weakness As there can be no allusion here to Hercules's love affairs or fits of insanity, Dickens must be referring to his customary good nature.
a baker's dozen Thirteen.
connubial missile Anything thrown by a wife at her husband.
trenchant Effective; its literal meaning of 'cutting' (Fr. 'trancher') seems also to apply here.
in an apothecary kind of way Sparingly, like a chemist with a prescribed ointment.
larcenous researches Search for something to steal.
Tar-water Infusion of tar in water.
elixir Once an imaginary drug capable of prolonging life.
boot-jack For pulling off tight boots.

imbruing Staining (with blood).
constitutional Characteristic.
copper-stick Stick for stirring clothes being washed in a copper
  container.
by easy friction By striking a match.

Chapter 3

On his way across the misty marshes Pip comes suddenly upon
another man in convict clothes who curses him and flees; after
watching his convict feed ravenously he mentions this figure
whom he has taken for the 'young man' used to frighten him on
the previous evening. Recognizing some old enemy in Pip's
description of the face, the convict attacks his leg-iron fiercely
with the file. While he is thus occupied Pip slips away home.

The chapter succeeds in building up the atmosphere of tension and mystery.

rimy Covered in frozen dew

Chapter 4

The tyranny exerted by Mrs Joe over her household is displayed
to the full in this episode: as an account of a Christmas celebra-
tion it is caricature in the extreme. The drastic cleaning, the
skimped breakfast, the discomfort of Sunday clothes, the annual
opening of the parlour and the front door, all rise to a climax in
the chorus of denunciation by a group of odious and hostile
adults of the one child present at a festival usually devoted to
children. This relentless persecution of Pip descends to the
lowest levels of attempted wit. The morning's sermon is dismissed in favour of a dissertation on being born a pig whose fate
at the hand of the butcher is, indeed, made to appear more
horrific than being 'brought up by hand' by Mrs Joe. For this
kind of salvation from the grave Pip is called upon to be grateful. Most of the time the youngster is holding on to a table-leg
for support in his dread of being found out but sustained by
spoonfuls of gravy handed down by Joe.

After a melodramatic reaction by Pumblechook to the tar-
water substituted by Pip for the brandy consumed by the convict, the tension created by Mrs Joe's visit to the pantry in search
of the missing pork pie is such that Pip rushes out of the room

only to find a file of soldiers at the door. No constable has turned up to arrest him for theft; instead a search party is on the track of his convict.

the Carols The mind reverts to that other so different Christmas described in Dickens's *A Christmas Carol*.
like monumental Crusaders Their fingers were as permanently crossed as the legs of some stone effigies in churches.
Sunday penitentials Best clothes, worn as if doing penance.
Accoucheur Policeman He had been 'arrested' at birth; 'accoucheur' is French for a male midwife.
chaise-cart A light carriage.
our friend overhead The parson, the clerk's place being in the lowest stage of a three-decker.
Ghost in Hamlet Well known for its sepulchral tones.
Richard the Third Another play of Shakespeare's, full of oratorical speeches.
alarmingly meditative Asking herself questions the answers to which would be embarrassing to Pip.

Chapter 5

Relieved to find that the handcuffs are not for a boy-thief but one of two escaped convicts, Pip, like everybody else, looks on as Joe repairs them. This takes two hours during which time the sergeant and Pumblechook exchange compliments. Joe and Pip are allowed to be spectators of the pursuit across the marshes. Carried on Joe's back the boy wonders whether, when his convict is caught, he will be seen as a traitor who has brought the soldiers on to his track.

Distant sounds of a fight reach their ears and eventually the two condemned men are arrested while struggling in a ditch. The second convict accuses the first of attempted murder, while the latter claims some credit for himself recapturing the other. After firing to signal their success the soldiers escort the prisoners to a landing-place for transport to the Hulks. The three villagers follow them all the way; Pip's convict, who has already exchanged a single significant look with the boy, explains to Joe that it is he who has eaten the stolen pie.

This is a chapter of strong contrasts: the warm kitchen and the cold marshes, the silent movements of the soldiers and the sudden outbursts of the fighting convicts, the intense darkness and the flicker of torches when the search is over, their different accents, one 'gentlemanly', the other coarse. There is symbolism in the closing lines: the chains anchoring the Hulk seem to make it in itself a prisoner; the extinguishing of the torches suggests the sealing of the convict's fate.

appreciative powers Pumblechook had applauded the sergeant's complimentary reference to Mrs Joe; later, after more of the corn-merchant's wine has circulated, he is addressed as 'a man that knows what's what'.

Hob and nob This variously spelt phrase usually expressed familiarity, especially between two drinkers.

Musical Glasses These contained graduated quantities of water and produced tunes when struck with the finger.

good sauce for a dinner The evening's enjoyment is greatly increased by the excitement aroused by the search for the convict.

turned pale in their account The suggestion that the 'pallor' of dusk is owing to sympathy with the fugitives is an example of 'natural fallacy', frequent in Dickens.

under arid conditions Having drunk nothing.

keeping the day Observing Christmas.

finger-post Sign-post.

thumping like a blacksmith Beating heavily. An odd echo of the forge.

'a Winder' Taking his breath away.

But if he had looked . . . more attentive This obscure sentence must be expressing the intensity of the convict's passing glance.

a saving remembrance The recollection in time that the pie had been given by Pumblechook to Mrs Joe.

Chapter 6

A very brief chapter dealing with two topics: (a) the reasons why Pip could not tell Joe about the file and (b) the different theories about how the convict could have robbed the pantry. Pip's decision to say nothing for fear of losing the confidence of his best friend is given an ironic turn by this adult self who writes that, innocent of wordly deception, he had discovered for himself the expediency of a 'white lie'.

Pumblechook's theory of the way the convict got in overrides other ideas. Wopsle provides the humour: having sat down so often on the way back and drying himself out before the fire, he is seen as both coatless and clueless. Dickensian exaggeration makes much of the wet patch and also of Pip's boots bumping against the stairs while he is being dragged off to bed.

in his lay capacity Not being a priest, he would be *sitting* in his clerk's pew.
slumberous offence He is offending by his very sleepiness.
the subject The missing pork-pie.

Chapter 7

An account of Pip's very elementary education and the lack of it in Joe through an upbringing which, as told by him, was even harsher than that of Pip. This is followed by the first phase of Pip's expectations, an invitation by the wealthy but eccentric Miss Havisham to visit her regularly and amuse her by 'playing'.

Dickens created a savage narrative out of his investigation of certain Yorkshire schools in *Nicholas Nickleby*; here he makes the most of some dame's school he may have come across in Kent. This grotesque setting, rendered even more absurd by Wopsle's dramatic recitations overhead, is sweetened by the presence of a fellow-orphan, Biddy, who begins her important part in Pip's life by teaching him what are now called the 'Three Rs'. His progress is demonstrated by a letter written to Joe, in Joe's presence, and in spite of many errors it is greatly admired by the unlettered blacksmith. The elder Gargery, also a blacksmith but a drunkard, apparently was the cause of Joe's ignorance, because he interrupted what little education his boy got by persistently fetching back his whole family soon after they had fled one of his alcoholic fits. In this novel the Past is sometimes made to appear even grimmer than the Present!

Joe, in the goodness of heart he inherited, it would seem, from his father, then reveals to Pip how he met his wife with her small dependent brother for whom he readily found room at the forge. All he can find now in her favour is her 'fine figure' for she is 'given to government', a peculiar phrase that echoes John Knox's 'monstrous regiment of women' but is merely used by Dickens for a weak pun most unlikely to be uttered by a child. Joe defends his meek acquiescence in the arbitrary rule of this 'master-mind' by expressing his fear of causing offence to any woman, in recollection of his ill-used mother.

Soon after eight Mrs Joe returns from market with Pumblechook in his trap to announce by mysterious stages Pip's 'good fortune'. The family benefactor has given Pip further cause to be grateful, first by recommending him to the great lady and then by offering to take him to his shop for the night in readiness for his first visit next morning. Before Pip goes, however, he is subjected to the most violent form of ablution of which his sister is capable. Suddenly parted from Joe the tearful youngster gets no enlightenment on his fate from the stars overhead.

'Below' This impossible inscription on any tombstone, thought up as an alternative to 'the Above', is an example of Dickens's playing with words, often to relieve depressing circumstances. This supposition is followed by an equally peculiar recollection (the author's own?) of always walking 'in the same' direction from his house.

six to seven Children were often employed during the day.

the National Debt Though then a mere fraction of today's amount, this financial burden is used to emphasize further the reduction to the very minimum of Pip's early 'expectations' in life.

Mark Antony's oration In Shakespeare's *Julius Caesar*, III,2.

Collins's 'Ode on the Passions' The relevant passage is:

> Revenge impatient rose
> He threw his blood-stain'd sword in thunder down;
> And with a withering look
> The war-denouncing trumpet took.

elaborated Dressed for the occasion.

those thieves, the nine figures The numerals. We can accept the extravagance of Pip being scratched by every letter he learnt and baffled by furtive changes of shape by the figures 1 to 9, but the note he writes looks more like a secret code than a childish epistle!

cipher Do sums in arithmetic (from an Arabic word meaning 'nought').

I ask no better Joe in his turn is hiding something (his illiteracy) from his young friend.

with a modest patronage Like a scholar condescending to a pupil.

keep the pot a-biling Contribute to the family livelihood.

purpleleptic He means 'apoplectic'.

divorced her in favour of . . . Treasury A strange idea for a child; yet Dickens preserved a childhood memory of the word 'government' used for those holding public office.

comes the Mogul Behaves like an autocrat; from the Mogul Emperors of India.

a Buster An overpowering person (obsolete).

Pompeyed Pampered, as already explained.

Mooncalfs Idiots (like Joe and Pip). From an abortion believed to have been caused by the moon.

Chapter 8

After a night in a room under the tiles Pip first becomes familiar with the combined flavour of seeds and the corduroys of seedsmen and then is struck by a curious chain of watchful inactivity on the part of the local tradesmen; only a group of rustics could be seen 'poring' over the watchmaker actually at work 'poring' over his desk. After a skimpy breakfast rendered even less enjoyable by a string of oral sums propounded to him by the egregious Pumblechook, Pip is taken to the house of Miss Havisham which resembles a prison from the outside. As he is being conducted to the lady of the 'manor-house' by a pretty but proud girl of his own age he notices the brewery now disused but probably the source of the family wealth. She leads him by candle-light (although outside it is broad day) through dark passages and ushers him into the room occupied by Miss Havisham where she leaves him to be interviewed. The once-neglected bride (so much is known outside) lives on, wearing her wedding dress and surrounded by her possessions kept in their original places. Like the clocks, stopped at the same hour (by her own hand), Time has stood still in this mouldering apartment. After examining Pip closely she makes an extraordinary request to him to 'play'. Dumbfounded, but mindful of his sister's threat – 'he had better play there' – he excuses himself and is told to summon the girl whose name, Estella, he has to shout into the prevailing darkness.

Having been reminded by Miss Havisham of sights he had once seen, a waxen effigy and a disinterred skeleton, he pauses in his account of that day to wonder if, were the sunlight to penetrate, it would turn her and her dress to dust, as happens to bodies that have been dug up. After Pip has been beaten at cards by Estella, contemptuous throughout, the corpse-like figure requests him to return in six days' time. He is further humiliated by Estella when she is told to supply him with food and drink on departure; thus fortified against continuing injustices, he explores the outhouses and is further tormented by a glimpse of Estella, whom he now admires, and terrified by a brief vision of Miss Havisham hanging from a beam. Estella eventually reappears to let him out of the main gate, taunting him for his tears. Finding no one in the shop he sets off on the four-mile walk home, painfully conscious of his new status as a 'common labouring boy'.

farinaceous Mealy.
those jails Even seed pods provide a further allusion to prison life.
a mortifying and penitential character Stinting his food in order to subdue the desires of the flesh.

transfixed A very apt word for the state of arrested development around him.

But, when she was gone . . . counteraction Written doubtless with the author's own early experiences in mind.

Irish hunter A horse.

those recluses The abandoned casks, with their faint odour from better days, may be intended as symbolic of the 'recluse' within, or possibly a hit at religious orders.

she should have no fair reason He would put on a bold face and ignore her as he passed.

Chapter 9

After severe punishment by his sister for his reticence about his encounter with Miss Havisham, which he explains to the reader as reluctance to betray the lady or her niece, Pip wildly invents a fairy-tale picture in mockery of Pumblechook's questions, the only true detail being the use of candlelight all day. It is also the only item that Pumblechook, who has to admit that he has never personally met the lady, can confirm.

Joe in turn is amazed at this fantastic revelation but in a quiet moment Pip explains that it has all been made up. Rebuked for telling lies, Pip blames it on his consciousness of being 'common'; not quite clear about the real meaning of this word Joe lectures the boy on the importance of not seeking to become 'uncommon' by falsehoods. He should ask forgiveness in his prayers and never do it again. Pip declares that this day has been the turning point in his life.

monstrosity An abnormal child.

aggravated The accepted word today is 'exasperated'.

caparisoned coursers Horses with covering cloths.

the father of lies Traditionally the Devil.

as being done intentional Not accidentally.

the first link Another hint of captivity – by Fate.

Chapter 10

In his ambition to become uncommon Pip asks Biddy to teach him all she knows, to supplement the almost total lack of education in the quite farcical school of Wopsle's great-aunt.

One evening Pip, commanded by his sister to accompany Joe home from the Three Jolly Bargemen, becomes an object of great interest to a stranger in the pub. Having learnt the boy's name and relationship, the latter gives him some mysterious glances and stirs his drink – with a file. To add to Pip's amazement, when Joe rises to go this man presents Pip with a new shilling wrapped in paper which proves on arrival home to be two pound notes. These are promptly consigned by his miserly sister to a pot on top of a cupboard.

Harder to bear is the reopening of his connection with anyone so 'common' as a convict. The possible reappearance of the file haunts him (though the impact is less disastrous than that of the later reappearance of the borrower of the file himself).

luminous conception Bright idea.
chalk scores Pub reckonings.
stiff company Standoffish.
give it out Announce the psalm in church.
ophthalmic steps Eye treatment.
old discomfiture His wet trousers after the chase (Chapter 6).

Chapter 11

On his second visit to Miss Havisham Pip meets further strange characters. He is told to wait a summons in a different room in the presence of three women and a man who seem to be watching him while engaged in desultory and rather gloomy gossip. On the way up Estella first strikes him to lower his opinion of her, then they meet Jaggers, the lawyer, who is on the way down on what proves to be Miss Havisham's birthday, the reason for the group of toadying relatives visiting her. Having said he is willing to work he is sent to what was the dining-room at the wedding, with a long table on which still moulders the feast, spiders spinning their webs round the wedding cake. After telling him that she will be laid on the table at her death, she makes Pip walk her about.

Estella is called for and reappears with the relatives who conduct a hypocritical conversation with their rich kinswoman, after which each is shown the place at the table he or she is to occupy when they come to feast (their eyes) on her corpse. The previous day's routine is now followed: he loses at cards, is given some food and left to roam the garden where he comes across a boy of his own age who insists on fighting him with due observance of the rules. To his own surprise Pip knocks him down but the boy is a glutton for punishment, which Dickens gives him in full measure. Whether Estella has seen his exploit or not, at his departure she offers him her cheek to kiss. His pleasure is alloyed by the thought that this is another piece of condescension. Night has fallen when he reaches home: instead of Estella's candle there are the light-house beam and the gleam from the forge.

pervaded Here it means 'traversed', while 'traversed' in the next line means 'passed along'.
inwardly crying for her Infatuated with her.
épergne Centre piece for a dinner table.
sal volatile Ammonia for fainting fits.

Chapter 12

On his next visit Pip is relieved to find no form of punishment is to be inflicted on him for his treatment of the boy he is later to form a close friendship with, Herbert Pocket. A new development is a wheelchair in which he pushes Miss Havisham round her limited domain. He is to be on duty now every other day, an arrangement which is to continue for several months, rewarded with no money, only his dinner. Estella grows prettier and even more capricious, to Miss Havisham's delight. At home Pip's future is discussed by Mrs Joe and the unctuous Pumblechook, and then one day Miss Havisham wishes to see Pip apprenticed.

If there is one scene more extraordinary than the singing of Joe's anvil song by Pip and the two ladies of Satis it is Mrs Joe's violent reaction to not being invited to visit the big house. Another chapter reaches its conclusion in the dark outside the forge, whither Joe and Pip have been driven.

myrmidons Officious servants. Originally Achilles' warriors.
suborned Bribed.
the family features The 'foreshortened' face of their young relative.
Old Clem Saint Clement. Better known as the patron saint of tanners.
an appropriate passenger Another extravagant lie.

Chapter 13

Leaving Mrs Joe at Pumblechook's, Joe accompanies Pip to Satis House, where Estella admits them and leads the way to Miss Havisham's room. Although the awe-struck Joe persists in speaking only to Pip, Miss Havisham hands him in business-like fashion twenty-five guineas as a fee for taking Pip as an apprentice. This sum she says the boy has earned working for her. On the way back Joe, reeling with 'astonishment', is yet shrewd enough to invent compliments from the great lady to his wife and then pretends that the money has been given not to him but to her.

The hypocritical Pumblechook claims real credit for this transaction and, acting as if he were ultimately responsible, declares Pip must be immediately bound apprentice. He drags his young victim to the court house as if he had a criminal in charge; then, after the simple procedure of signing the indentures over, the party, augmented by the Hubbles and Wopsle, dine sumptuously at the Blue Boar, paying for it out of the apprenticeship fee. Not at all enjoying the 'festival' the young apprentice ends another late night with a strong aversion to the blacksmith's trade.

like the Great Seal of England Large and round.
pattens Wooden overshoes worn as protection against mud.
Cleopatra The famous Egyptian queen who, when summoned to appear before Mark Antony, put on her most ravishing attire and captivated him.
epitaph Joe composes an impromtu couplet like that 'struck out' as an epitaph for his father, in Chapter 7.
sut Soot.
a perfect sausage-shop of fetters A great length of chains.
Rantipole Noisy rascal, inappropriate as applied to Pip.
hard-bake Almond toffee.
Collins's Ode See note in Chapter 7.

Chapter 14

Another brief chapter on a painful topic (cf. Chap. 6). Pip is oppressed by a sense of disenchantment with his home and Joe's forge, his prospects seeming as bleak as the landscape. However, he never murmurs and now attributes the completion of his apprenticeship to the good influence of Joe. The thought of Estella seeing him at work in such humble surroundings fills him with constant dread and an increasing sense of shame.

retributive Punishment *is* retributive.
solemn opening The annual event at Christmas for guests to dinner.
Now the reality was in my hold Now I was apprenticed.

Chapter 15

Pip passes on as much of his education as he can to Joe, to make him less objectionable to Estella. Most of the information vanishes from Joe's mind like the smoke from his pipe, while Pip finds images of Estella and her mistress in various aspects of the landscape. He eventually suggests a half-holiday which Orlick the journeyman, now introduced to the story with a strong dislike for Pip, also demands. The granting of this is scorned by Mrs Joe, who by screaming at Orlick provokes a quarrel between the two men, in which the journeyman is defeated.

Pip finds Estella gone abroad to a finishing school and then comes across Wopsle, with whom he returns home via Pumblechook's, where Pip is subjected to a Wopsle recitation; the two meet Orlick on their way to the village, hear the warning by gun of a convict's escape and, alerted by excitement at the inn reach the forge to find Mrs Joe has been paralysed by a blow from some intruder.

lay-figure Wooden model of the human body; here indicating a passive partnership in a stage dialogue.

a set of shoes Horseshoes, handiwork of a blacksmith.

oncommon Harking back to the argument in Chapter 9.

Cain The killer of his brother Abel.

Wandering Jew A legendary figure condemned to go on living after he had taunted Christ on His way to the Cross.

locomotively When moving about.

a perfect Fury and a complete success A first-rate impersonation of one of the three Furies, merciless instruments of the gods sent to punish the guilty.

parenthetical interruptions Joe's mild entreaties to Orlick to 'let her alone' as indicated by their insertion in *brackets*.

neither expressive nor ornamental Neither part of his facial expression nor an attractive feature.

George Barnwell *The London Merchant, or the History of George Barnewell* by Lillo, was acted in 1731.

murdering a near relation This echo of an old play is rather artificially used as a foretaste of what awaits Pip at the forge.

become my benefactor Make me his heir, so asking to be murdered.

turnpike lamp Light on the barrier placed across a road on which a toll had to be paid.

a suggestive one to me Reminder of his meeting with a convict.

ill-requited Murdered.

meditating aloud Reciting again the lines of the play.

Camberwell London borough south of the Thames.

Bosworth Field Scene of the final battle in Shakespeare's *Richard III* where the king puts up a desperate fight.
Glastonbury The reference is more likely to the hanging and quartering of the last abbot than to the death and burial of King Arthur.

Chapter 16

The only clue to the identity of the attacker is a convict's leg-iron which has been filed. Pip concludes this must be the one from which his convict freed himself; it would have been picked up by the assailant, who could be Orlick or perhaps the man who showed Pip the file. After debating whether he should finally reveal his secret Pip decides to await the result of the investigation by the Bow Street Runners whose incompetence in this novel is a gross exaggeration, particularly in their suspicions of Joe.

The now permanent invalid is able to communicate only by writing, in her case as imperfect as Joe's ability to read. The problem is solved by Biddy joining the household; she discovers the meaning of the T-shaped symbol drawn by Mrs Joe on the slate: it is Orlick's hammer intended as a summons which becomes a daily occurrence, marked by a puzzling change in Mrs Joe's attitude to one of anxious concern for one with whom she has had such a vicious quarrel.

snuff Part of the wick not consumed after the candle has been snuffed.
Bow Street men The famous 'runners', so called after London's chief police court who acted as detectives until 1829.
conquered a confirmed habit of living Dickensian circumlocution for 'died at last'.

Chapter 17

Pip's annual visit to Satis House on his birthday becomes an unchanging ritual whereas Biddy undergoes a remarkable change in Pip's eyes. He is impelled to express his admiration for the way in which she both manages the household and keeps level with him in his studies, limited as they are. During a walk with her on the lonely marshes Pip confesses his discontent with his 'common' way of life, an attitude inspired by Estella; he even admits the desirability of loving Biddy instead of Estella, a possibility which the sensible girl calmly dismisses. When they meet the sinister Orlick she tells Pip that the journeyman, now a regular visitor to the house, is showing an interest in her, but when Pip is indignant she points out that this is hardly his concern.

This period of oscillation in his attitude between settling down to a steady if humble life with Joe and Biddy and hankering after vague romantic expectations associated with Miss Havisham is soon to be terminated.

reciprocated my good intentions Similarly wished me ill.

Chapter 18

Pip is at the inn with Joe listening with the other customers to Wopsle making a dramatic reading out of a newspaper report of a murder trial when a stranger, whom Pip remembers seeing at Satis House, first displays his legal knowledge by refuting the group's readiness to condemn the prisoner in the report as guilty and then asks for the local blacksmith and his apprentice. Giving his name as Jaggers, and preferring to speak to them privately, he accompanies them to the forge; there he begins by asking Joe what compensation he will expect for losing his apprentice (to which the indignant reply is – nothing) and goes on to explain to Pip that a benefactor, whose identity must remain a secret until deliberately revealed, personally wishes him to be given an education fitting him to inherit the estate. Jaggers 'mentions' Matthew Pocket as a possible tutor and then, after presenting Pip with twenty guineas with which to buy suitable clothes, angers Joe by repeating his offer of compensation.

The double connection of Jaggers and Pocket with Satis House makes Pip henceforth suspect that Miss Havisham is his benefactor. After the lawyer's departure the news of Pip's prospects arouses mixed feelings in the kitchen: sadness in the hearts of his two best friends, a guilty sense in his own of escaping from 'commonness', betrayed in his wish not to be seen in the village in his new clothes. As Joe and Biddy converse beneath his window Pip goes to sleep oppressed by a new sense of loneliness.

Timon of Athens ... Coriolanus Title parts in two of Shakespeare's plays, respectively a misanthrope and an aristocrat turned traitor.

Holdfast Keeping one's word, in spite of temptation. Actually a dog's name.
hackney-coach Carriage for hire.
a darker picture ... than electoral ignorance.

Chapter 19

This comprehensive chapter, covering Pip's last six days in his old home, ranges in feeling from deep pathos to downright farce; there is some blunt speaking in the dialogue and occasional subtle irony in the description. Days that dawn bright with prospective fortune close with evenings of increasingly isolated self-pity. Typical of Pip's mixed and rather hypocritical attitude is first his solitary farewell stroll in which he is overtaken by Joe and then his decision to meet the coach alone. The substance of his discussions with Joe and Biddy is his regret that Joe has not responded to his efforts to improve him and so fit him for something higher than the blacksmith's trade, of which Pip is now ashamed. Biddy's protest that Joe might himself be too proud to change his way of life angers Pip, who accuses her of envying him his good fortune.

This sad misunderstanding is followed by comic extremes: Pip's discovery of the social effects of the possession of wealth is grossly over-played in the new-found obsequiousness of Trabb and the utter reversal by Pumblechook of his treatment of a poor little orphan, now that he has expectations. Pip is overwhelmed with wine, good food and endlessly repeated blandishments but is sufficiently alert to avoid directly investing any capital in the corn business.

After three more days devoid of incident Pip spends his last day on a visit to Miss Havisham in his new suit, secretly donned beforehand at Pumblechook's; she wickedly uses the knowledge of Pip's prospects gained from Jaggers to insinuate that she is really the 'fairy godmother' he thinks her to be. A sleepless night is followed by a hurried breakfast, and Pip says farewell at the forge but he bursts into tears as he comes to the village signpost. With each change of horses he ponders whether to change his mind and return; eventually with the rising of the mist he looks forward to what London has to offer.

press Cupboard.
the rich man See the Gospel of St Mark x,24–5.

alone A selfish impulse, as shown by Joe following him.

obscurely The reader is reminded of Gray's *Elegy Written in a Country Churchyard*, 'Where heaves the turf in many a mouldering heap.'

a gallon of condescension Pip pours some of it out in this chapter.

plump Abruptly.

for the elevation of her spirits This expresses the shallowness of the sentiment he is about to put into words.

waiving its application In modern terms 'present company excepted'.

tiding it out in a flowing manner Unfolding it in a wave formation.

rubbed me out Saw me out while rubbing his hands respectfully.

Mother Hubbard's dog From the nursery rhyme.

the Barnwell Parlour The scene of Wopsle's recitation.

had round Ordered to be brought.

No Thoroughfares of Pork Inedible parts, formerly given to Pip at home.

flaccid Flabby.

noble-minded Pip has shown forgiveness in drinking his cruel sister's health.

vastness and distinctness Ironic for an attitude limited in scope and indecisive in effect.

slumberously Drunkenly.

crook Bend.

I should want To make use of them.

finger-post Signpost with a pointing finger.

If I had cried before . . . then If I had given way to better feelings Joe would have come with me to the coach.

Revision questions on the First Stage

1 Describe and account for the companionship of Pip and Joe.

2 Mention the various consequences of the convict's escape.

3 Relate Pip's experiences at Satis House.

4 Describe the relationship at different times between Pip and Biddy.

5 In how many ways is Pip affected by his good fortune?

6 Write short sketches of Wopsle and Orlick.

7 Show how Dickens creates an atmosphere of fear in any *two* or *three* of these chapters.

8 What aspects of the story so far do you find humorous and why?

Assignments

1 Write an account of any situation in a book you have read where the narrator is isolated and frightened.

2 Give a picture of family life or social life as it is presented in any book which deals with the past.

3 Write about the presentation of childhood in a book you are studying.

4 Describe anything grotesque in a book you have read recently, bringing out its particular qualities.

5 Write about the author's powers of description in the particular book you are studying.

Chapter 20

Pip's poor first impression of the great city is made still more dismal by Jaggers's office. Impatient at the lawyer's delayed arrival, Pip goes sight-seeing: he flees the revolting spectacle of Smithfield meat-market to find himself outside Newgate Prison where trials are being held. Refusing the offer, at a price, of a front seat at court, he is shown the door through which the condemned emerge on their way to execution. Jaggers is not yet back, so Pip starts off on a second tour, only to find that his guardian's legal services are in great demand, especially by shady characters. After dealing summarily with these on-the-spot clients, including a heavily accented Jew, Jaggers, while munching a hasty sandwich, tells Pip where he is to be accommodated and the amount of his allowance. He is taken to Herbert Pocket's rooms in Barnard's Inn by Wemmick, the clerk.

ravel Tangle; hence 'unravel'.
Cross Keys Dickens himself arrived here from Kent in 1822.
hammer-cloth Cloth covering the driver's seat.
harrow Timber frame with iron teeth, normally used to break up soil; here to deter 'amateur footmen' from taking a free ride.
eccentrically patched like a broken head This is more puzzle than description; possibly odd panes of glass give a false perspective to higher buildings.
detrimental mastery Control through knowledge of guilty secrets.
the Lord Chief Justice's proprietor The 'minister of justice' (some kind of beadle) who offered to display him.

Little Britain A street.
Cag-Maggerth Cagmag (offal) is made to rhyme with Jaggers (Jewish pronunciation) as a contrast of opposites.
the Bull He tolled the bell in the rhyme 'The Death of Cock Robin'.
Barnard's Inn A former Inn of Chancery (a junior institution to the Inns of Court) which provided rooms, but not as dilapidated as Dickens's description in the next chapter.
outrunning the constable Spending more than the legal amount.

Chapter 21

An unfavourable impression of Wemmick's rather wooden personal appearance is surpassed by the quite extravagant denigration of 'Barnard's Inn', the name which at first suggested a hotel to Pip. The incredible state of dilapidation is in keeping with the clerk's own dehumanized behaviour as a London type. Wemmick leaves Pip to await the return of a Mr Herbert Pocket after half an hour. The latter explains in his apology that he has been purchasing fruit (a commodity relished in the country) for his guest. Each is surprised to recognize his boyhood opponent in the one-sided fight at Satis House.

post office of a mouth A pillar-box slit.
Holborn Hill Now replaced by a Viaduct (1869).
hotel The word 'inn', now describing a hostelry, was once used also of a private dwelling, especially a nobleman's. The Four Inns of Court became a university of the law, with nine subsidiary Inns of Chancery, of which Barnard's Inn was one, named after a fifteenth-century principal, Lionel Barnard; the hall is now part of the Mercers' School.
Haven Place of refuge ('any port in a storm'); sarcastic for the wretched buildings just described.
frouzy mourning Dingy funeral attire.
forlorn creation Pip assumes first that there has been some medieval curse and then that some eighteenth-century landlord is responsible.
strewed ashes on its head As a sign of repentance.
'Try Barnard's Mixture' Dickens cannot resist a tilt at advertisements of cheap brands of tobacco.
So imperfect . . . expectations A miserable slum instead of a fine residence. Dickens is determined to exaggerate the difference between romantic hopes and grim reality.
retirement Wemmick's mistake is in thinking Pip finds the scarcity of tenants a reminder of rural solitudes. Herbert is to speak of his rooms as 'retired'.
except at last As a final parting, or a funeral?
looking out On to the little square.

Covent Garden Market For two centuries the main market for fruit and vegetables.

I am rather bare here My rooms are scantily furnished.

we shan't fight As this is spoken before recognition, it meets the defintion of 'dramatic irony'.

One, Two First one, then the other. The pause leads to the recognition.

Chapter 22

This is a chapter of revelations. Pip explains his first visit to Satis House and Herbert in turn reveals that he has already been tried out as a possible suitor for Estella and failed; this he now regards as an escape from Miss Havisham's scheme of revenge on the male sex. Pip learns that Jaggers, as the lady's lawyer, had proposed Herbert's father, Miss Havisham's out-of-favour cousin, as his tutor. He then volunteers full information on his own background and asks Herbert to coach him in correct behaviour. As Herbert has asked to be called by his Christian name, Pip gives his as 'Philip' which Herbert so dislikes that he suggests 'Handel' instead, from the composer of the popular 'Harmonious Blacksmith'. After dinner, supplied by the local 'coffee-house' to the 'Inn' and served in a 'gipsy' manner Herbert tells the story (punctuated by parenthetical words of advice on table manners) of Miss Havisham.

When she inherited the larger portion of her wealthy brewer father's fortune her wicked half-brother (by a second marriage) was jealous and schemed to make her fall in love with an adventurer who not only got her to accept him as a husband but, against the advice of Matthew Pocket, persuaded her to buy out her brother's share for an extravagant sum, after which both villains vanished and came to bad ends. When the bridegroom failed to turn up Miss Havisham was so shocked that she completely, down to the last detail, 'arrested' life at Satis. Herbert's careful reference to the secrecy surrounding Pip's good fortune reinforces the latter's belief that Miss Havisham is responsible for his 'expectations'. These indeed are exceeded by the airy ambitions of the tutor's son of making his mark in the world of insurance and investment, though they are soon discounted by the reality of an unpaid job in a 'counting-house' where Herbert 'looks about him' for the opportunity to make some 'capital'.

The companionship of 'Handel', whose expectations lie in the future, and Herbert, who thinks of his as about to be realized, looks set to be a pleasant one though in the silent night Pip's mind wanders to the faraway forge kitchen. One Monday he accompanies Herbert to his home in Hammersmith and is there introduced to Mrs Pocket, whose concentration on the book she is reading in the garden renders her largely oblivious to her large family 'tumbling' round her (a footstool being concealed under her skirt). The father, Matthew Pocket, emerges to meet his pupil with the resigned air of one who has ceased to nurse any expectations.

confounded his intention with his execution Imagined he had given Pip the beating he intended for him. Compare this with Pip's 'established conviction' on the next page.
conquered languor Habit of reacting passively to misfortunes.
with no old people by Especially the heartless adults of his early years.
circumjacent Adjacent on all sides (obsolete); the rest of the room.
pastureless and shifty Unconnected with a meal and serving an ad hoc purpose only.
the waiter The reader is left wondering what went on in the mind of this intriguing character.
congelation Congealing into a solid form.
cut into the Direction Join the board of directors.
incipient giants Financiers in the making.
'Change The Royal Exchange.
more enduring lamentation i.e. their crying lasted longer.

Chapter 23

Matthew Pocket, by nature as unaffected as his son, is the opposite of his wife who was nurtured from birth with artificial expectations of an aristocratic existence by her dead father. He himself obtained a knighthood by virtue of his small part in some trivial ceremony, while suspecting that his own father, and Mrs Pocket's grandfather, had been cheated of a baronetcy. Married when both were young and inexperienced the Pockets left the control of their extraordinary household to their staff of servants who now lived as well as their employers upstairs. Pocket, educated at Harrow and Cambridge, had found it necessary to earn a living by giving private lessons, sometimes boarding his pupils.

Two residents are the boorish Drummle and the more studious Startop. At dinner Pip is placed next to a Mrs Coiler and finds her flow of stupid conversation a distraction from his personal attention to his table manners – a rather superfluous precaution in view of Mr Pocket's peculiar but characteristic habit of violently pulling his hair over any affliction – on this occasion a report from the kitchen that the beef is missing. This farcical banquet is followed by the traditional but even more farcical presentation of the children, managed in desperate fashion by the two nurses. When one little girl displays good sense in taking nutcrackers from the grasp of an infant sprawling on the lap of Mrs Pocket, she is subjected to a harangue from her mother for 'interfering', countered by another hair-raising protest by her husband; after Mrs Pocket has taken the baby away and left her husband with the remaining five, he rather ineffectively bribes each of them with a shilling and sends them to play somewhere else.

After an interlude on the river where each of the three students does some rowing, supper leads to further extravagant behaviour: when a housemaid reports that the cook is drunk Pocket goes to see for himself and on his return is scolded by his wife for believing a tell-tale.

Collapsing on to a sofa, the master of the house can only mutter 'Goodnight, Mr Pip'. And once more our hero ends a chapter by getting into bed sobered by his experiences of the day.

accidental Knighted by chance and not as the result of a set purpose.

storming . . . at the point of the pen Composing a masterful passage: mock metaphor from a knight with drawn sword.

mount to the Woolsack Become Lord Chancellor.

roof himself in with a mitre Become a bishop.

forelock A lock of hair on the front of the head. To take Time by it was to anticipate the proper time for action.

Grinder Crammer (long obsolete).

blades Young gallants. Dickens puns on their connection with a grindstone.

'read' with divers Helped various students in their work.

installation Ceremonial investment of someone with high office. A mock pretentious word for Pip's first night.

elect Chosen race (of aristocrats).

engaged in carving Presumably some other course than the beef!

a dissipated page A squanderer who was no longer wholly a 'boy in buttons'; had he used the missing ones as coins?

affront She saw interference as an insult to her grandfather who might have been a baronet.

billeted by Nature on Given as children to.
Missionary way As if talking to some heathen race.
a Dying Gladiator Compare with the well-known description in
  Byron's *Childe Harold's Pilgrimage*, IV, cxl.
Mr Pip Herbert's 'Handel' is known to his father as 'Pip', by way of
  Miss Havisham.

Chapter 24

Mr Pocket looks like being an exemplary tutor. Pip suggests
keeping on his bedroom at Barnard's Inn where he will be able
to benefit from Herbert's company. To buy the necessary furniture he approaches Jaggers and, after the far-reaching catechism which the lawyer regards as the 'professional' way of
arriving at an agreement, is allowed to draw twenty pounds.
When Jaggers has gone out Wemmick explains to Pip how crafty
and successful his employer is and shows him members of the
small staff dealing with clients; he identifies the two notorious
criminals, the plaster-casts of whose faces, made after execution,
had drawn Pip's shocked attention on his first visit; then he
displays some of the 'portable property' in the form of brooches,
rings and other jewellery left to him as grim legacies by some of
those about to be hanged.

   Wemmick invites Pip to visit him at his home in Walworth and
recommends that if he dines with Jaggers he should take special
notice of the house-keeper. Finally he takes him to watch Jaggers 'at it' in court, ruthlessly cross-examining a witness and
striking awe indiscriminately into Bench and dock.

affectionate apostrophe Intimate form of address.
Bounceable He exaggerated.
Walworth A South London suburb.
in the murderous sense Another murderer.

Chapter 25

While Pip's fellow students are, one loutish, the other rather
effeminate, his closest friend is Herbert. Mr Pocket's disagreeable relatives (first met at Satis) put in an appearance, if only to
show their dislike of Pip who, however, is making good progress
in his studies while living somewhat extravagantly. He arranges
to meet Wemmick at the office in Little Britain and walk with
him to Walworth. On the way he is further enlightened on the

prospective dinner with Jaggers whose rooms are never locked and are in no danger of being burgled, such is the fear of him among the thieving community.

Wemmick's home is a small cottage with a miniature draw-bridge and a flagstaff; its garden produce guarantees ample food supplies in case of the 'castle' being besieged. Having walked down a devious path and reached the central 'bower' with its tiny lake and artificial fountain they enter the all-purpose room to meet Wemmick's father who is intensely proud of his son's ingenuity – in a world far removed from that of Jaggers. After the firing of the gun Pip is shown the collection of curios. Following a delightful supper, laid by the little maid who looks after the old man by day, Pip is shown to a little turret bedroom, from which next morning he observes Wemmick already up and busy. On the way back to the City Wemmick gradually resumes the wooden character he had long adopted when at work in Jaggers's office.

between the two places A five-mile stretch.
my deficiences In knowledge.
walking down to Walworth A mere two and a half miles.
Britannia metal A cheap alloy looking like silver.
not merely mechanically Not like the 'post-office' in Chapter 21.
distinguished razor Instrument of some notorious cut-throat.
brazen bijou Brass ring.

Chapter 26

Having invited Pip and his three friends to dinner, Jaggers leads them in person to his spacious rooms in Soho. The solid furniture includes a book-case filled with volumes on the law and a work-table covered with papers. The meal is served by the housekeeper while Jaggers sees to the general entertainment with the aid of a dumb-waiter. When the conversation turns to rowing, with the baring of arms to show muscle, Jaggers seizes his housekeeper's arm and makes her display both of her wrists, declaring that she has as strong a hand-grip as any he has known.

Jaggers's interest in Drummle leads to an argument about the borrowing of money, Startop having lent some to Drummle. The young men have become flushed with the wine but Drummle turns violent. Resenting being laughed at, he seizes a glass to throw at Startop when it is intercepted by Jaggers who then indicates that it is getting late. On the point of leaving Pip returns briefly to apologize for their behaviour and is told that, while Jaggers likes the look of Drummle, Pip must give him a wide berth.

jack-towel On a roller.
scraped the case Removed the dirt from his finger-nails, as if dismissing the last details of a case in court from his mind.
what kind of loops A hangman's noose.
amphibious way i.e. keeping close to the bank (Chapter 25).

Chapter 27

Biddy's letter announcing the arrival of Joe in London disturbs Pip's satisfaction at having redecorated the flat: this was at considerable expense, and he also enlisted the son of his washerwoman to be Boots in the diminutive hall off the staircase, and to introduce visitors. The two old friends briefly express their gladness at this reunion, but Joe's awkward behaviour, especially his antics in holding on to his hat, further embarrasses Pip when Herbert arrives; also when Joe gives his unfavourable opinion of the 'Inn' (note Biddy's reference in the letter to a 'Hotel').

The uneasy relationship that has developed between Pip and his erstwhile 'companion' is highlighted by Joe's swinging from the politeness of 'Sir' to the familiar 'Pip' and back again. The conscience of the blacksmith's former apprentice is pricked when he learns that the visit that has made him flinch has been undertaken to bring him personally the welcome news that Estella would like to see him. Joe immediately leaves for home after delivering a simple but dignified speech accepting the division between the life of a 'gentleman' and that of a tradesman. Joe further declares that henceforth he will be met by Pip (should the latter even desire it) only at the forge in his working clothes.

Pip is so touched that he recollects himself too late to overtake Joe who has disappeared. The reader is left wondering what he might have found to say.

sense of incongruity The exaggerated eccentricity of Joe's appearance, speech and actions may have seemed necessary to Dickens in order to embarrass Pip thoroughly for the snobbery that his ambition has developed towards his old home; his ambition, like that of Macbeth in the play referred to in this chapter, has been stimulated by external agencies – two ladies with witch-like propensities!

the refuse The least worthy of employment.
last patented Pump The one with the latest patented device.
Roscian renown Roscius was a famous Roman actor.
the highest tragic walk *Hamlet*, featuring the Ghost of Hamlet's father.
'Amen!' Wopsle's hecklers know his occupation as parish clerk.
the Avenger The boy gets this pseudonym from the passing phrase 'avenging phantom', possibly suggested by his 'haunting' Pip's existence, like some classical Fury tracking him down to destroy him.
Blacking Ware'us. See the reference under 'The author and his work'.
partings welded together This blacksmith has welded two ideas together: 'parting' as the separation of two friends, and 'parting' as a more definite division between classes.

Chapter 28

For his visit to Satis House Pip decides to stay overnight at the Blue Boar, wisely leaving his expensive page behind. Seen off by Herbert, he gets a painful reminder of the past in the form of two convicts travelling on the same coach, one of whom he recognizes as the mystery man who showed him the file (Chapter 10). He overhears this man, seated behind him, tell the other how he has faithfully passed on two pounds from Magwitch to a mere boy and, though Pip is now grown up, he leaves the coach at the first stopping-place in town. This chance encounter revives his childhood fears and creates a vague dread of further coincidental association with convicts. Firmly refusing the waiter's suggestion that Pumblechook should be invited he is shown a local paper in which appears a verbose article publicizing, while withholding names, the corn merchant's exclusive claim to be the earliest friend and benefactor of the young man alluded to as 'Telemachus'.

folding up my bank-notes Is this a curiously contrived anticipation of what Pip is to overhear on the coach?
slued A former alternative spelling of 'slewed', turned on its own axis.
Lifer Prisoner for life.
the Great Remonstrance Parliament's Grand Remonstrance to the King in 1641; the reference is to the day of Pip's being made an apprentice (Chapter 13).
Telemachus Son of Ulysses who grew up in his father's absence during

the war with Troy; while seeking Ulysses he was given advice by the goddess of wisdom in the person of Mentor, a friend of his father's.

Quinten Matsys Quentin Massys (1466–1530) was a Flemish painter who worked as a blacksmith (hence the allusion) before going to Antwerp.

VERB.SAP. Short for *verbum sapienti*, a word to the wise (is sufficient).

Chapter 29

Up early, Pip indulges in romantic dreams of himself married to Estella and restoring Satis House to its former grandeur, while admitting that his unalterable love for Estella is against reason. He finds Orlick on duty as gate-keeper, ready with sarcastic rejoinders. He makes his way to Miss Havisham's room where he sees her sitting as before, in the company of Estella. The latter is changed into such an elegant lady that he fails to recognize her at first. She in turn confesses to having observed a change in him.

They go for a walk in the garden and then the yard, Estella calm and dignified and strangely forgetful of earlier incidents, Pip the devoted admirer, conscious nevertheless of the false gentility she has inspired. She explains that she has no heart, the consequent lack of tenderness making her forget emotional links with the past. In a tormented state of mind, partly occasioned by a strange resemblance at times in Estella to some-one else, Pip returns with her to wheel Miss Havisham as he once did. The ghostly figure urges Pip repeatedly and passionately to love Estella. Jaggers arrives for dinner which is taken in another room; the lawyer explains that Miss Havisham never dines in company but lives on scraps.

When the strange meal (for four, including Sarah Pocket and served by one more of those domestics who makes a single appearance) is finished with, and the two gentlemen are left with the port, Jaggers maintains a characteristically pregnant reserve which continues throughout the game of whist (this time with Miss Havisham). The lawyer's skill with the cards hurts Pip far less than the chilling effect his presence has on his passionate regard for Estella. He spends a tearful night at the inn before returning to London where he is to meet Estella on her arrival there at a later date.

In a chapter charged with sentiment the tenderest reference is to Pip's omission to visit the forge.

Tag and Rag and Bobtail The rabble, e.g. escaped convicts. Note 'the
  tag-rag people' in Shakespeare's *Julius Caesar*, I,ii.
rewarded me With a kiss.
at your old post Behind the wheelchair.

Chapter 30

Leaving the inn early to avoid Pumblechook Pip becomes the
unwilling victim of the performance of Trabb's boy in mimic-
king a young gentleman of fashion, attended by a juvenile audience. Escaping to the outskirts of the town he is picked up by the
coach. Back in London he sends his page to the theatre in order
to be able to unburden himself, without being overheard, of his
love affair. Herbert's optimism helps to brighten Pip's lack of
confidence in his prospects (after all the involvement of Jaggers
is sufficient guarantee of reality). His friend then ventures to
suggest further that Pip free himself from his infatuation, only
to confide in his turn that he too is in love. The contrast is clearly
intentional; it is with someone *below* family expectations, whom
Herbert nevertheless intends to marry when he has acquired
some 'capital'. When Pip comes upon Wopsle's playbill in his
pocket they decide to see the actor's performance in Hamlet –
the day having begun with a piece of street entertainment!

the right sort of man The rarity of this kind of appointment makes for
  plenty of work for a Jaggers in dealing with the *wrong* sort.
antechamber to the keyhole An apartment leading to the main room,
  the activities of whose occupants could be viewed *through* the keyhole.
with a magnifying glass Looking for minor faults to criticize.
the dustman He finds ample refuse in the dustbins of this improvident
  household.
marine-store Selling miscellaneous goods, originally to supply ships.

Chapter 31

Pip and Herbert find increasing amusement in this farcical (not
to say improbable) production of which various episodes seem
extravagant burlesques of scenes familiar to most readers.
Wopsle as Prince is greeted by a stream of witticisms from the
audience, particularly from a man in the gallery (identified later
by Wopsle as employed for this purpose by the therefore doubly
treacherous King Claudius!). Seeking to avoid the old acquaintance they have been laughing at, they are intercepted by his

dresser with a message from 'Mr Waldengarver'. While Wopsle struggles out of his black stage garments, the two young men think up complimentary epithets for his performance. Out of kindness they invite him to supper, an occasion utilized by him to inflict on them a lengthy account of his ambitions in the theatrical world. After all this Pip understandably endures a nightmare.

arrival in Denmark Taking their seats and seeing before them the stage setting of Elsinore.
the place of reference The cue.
suggestive of a state of mortality Indicating that the actor playing the part is only human (like the irritating cough).
'turn over' Difficult to do when the copy is wrapped round a truncheon.
a person of the utmost importance . . . judged This must be the part of Osric, who acted as a referee in the duel between Hamlet and Laertes: 'A hit, a palpable hit!'.
crawling between earth and heaven See Hamlet's speech in II,ii: 'O, what a rogue and peasant slave am I!'
not to saw the air thus From Hamlet's advice to the visting players: 'do not saw the air too much with your hand.'
service A slip by the parish clerk.
Claudius The King employs others to destroy Hamlet.

Chapter 32

A letter from Estella giving the time of her arrival in London throws Pip into a feverish state of expectation. Turning up hours beforehand at the coach station he encounters Wemmick and is persuaded to spend part of the waiting interval on a visit to Newgate Prison. The clerk makes contact through the bars with cases known to him including a 'colonel' about to be hanged for forgery from whom he receives as a parting gift the promise of a pair of pigeons.

In conversation with Wemmick and the turnkeys Pip learns more of the domination exerted by Jaggers in the criminal world; but he is also conscious of the contrast between the prison atmosphere and the ethereal beauty of Estella.

his post-office in an immovable state Without opening his mouth.
full blow Full bloom, as if at a flower show. This analogy with the work of a gardener is given a logical conclusion farther on.
quantum Specified amount, or fixed fee.

useless measures Approaching a subordinate.
real A genuine ring.
Coiner Maker of counterfeit money.
of minor abilities Less overpowering.

Chapter 33

Following instructions brought by Estella Pip orders a private coach to take them to Richmond (Surrey), meanwhile finding the least shabby room in the inn and ordering tea. Estella's manner is much more pleasing, though still puzzling, with more than a hint that she regards both of them as puppets in the hands of others. She is to stay with a lady who can introduce her to London society. Pip learns about the way he is being defamed by his tutor's jealous relations, and notices the bitterness with which Estella vengefully gloats over their discomfiture (because of Pip's good fortune). During the conversation he ventures on a compliment and kisses her hand.

After the bill for a most unsatisfactory and dilatory tea has been paid (from Estella's purse) they leave in the coach, unfortunately passing Newgate Prison, which leads them to compare notes about Jaggers. At Hammersmith Pip points out the Pockets' house; at Richmond Estella is received into an old house that has evidently seen the splendours of an earlier generation. Returning to Hammersmith Pip finds Mr Pocket out lecturing (on domestic economy, of all things) and Mrs Pocket ordering the baby to be put to bed while herself absorbed in her book of titles.

Our lesson Information acquired in a geography lesson.
slightingly Scornful of their two destinies.
as if it must be done Obeying instructions rather than behaving
  voluntarily.
impostor The insomniac Camilla (Chapter 11).
magic clue His napkin.
glare of gas Gas was already in use for lighting London streets, but as it
  must have been still daylight, perhaps this was an 'escape'.
solitaire Neck-tie.
to take as a tonic The humour of this is rather forced.

Chapter 34

Pip pauses in his narrative to describe the psychological effect of his expectations (of an estate) on himself (his attitude to Joe and

Biddy) and on Herbert (his extravagant way of life proving a bad example). They join an expensive but otherwise purposeless club and stay up late at night drinking. As Herbert insists on paying his own way he sees his hopes of realizing 'capital' receding. They follow the fashion of young fops in spending lavishly for little of substance in return. Herbert seems to achieve nothing at his poky little office, which he leaves daily for an equally profitless call at Lloyds – as profitless as Pip's continued employment of a stupid 'Boots'.

Their mode of dealing with increasing debts is, after a celebratory dinner, to take out a heap of stationery, compile a fresh list of sums owed, check it again with the original bills, solemnly tick off each item and finally allow a 'margin' outside the total expenditure. This practice, initiated by Pip and regarded by Handel as proof of the former's 'administrative genius' usually has a soothing effect, inducing what is now often defined as a state of 'euphoria'.

One evening this state of mind is interrupted by a letter requesting Pip's attendance at his sister's funeral.

apron Leather cover for the legs of the driver of a carriage.

Chapter 35

The death of Pip's sister shocks him into more frequent recollection of her, softened by time. On the day of the funeral he finds the mourners in full black as prescribed by Trabb, who also as undertaker, organizes the procession of people in twos, displaying their handkerchiefs, on the way to the churchyard. They are greatly admired by the village. Irritated throughout by the persistent attentions of the old hypocrite Pumblechook, Pip sits down to dinner with Joe and Biddy in an atmosphere of restraint.

Pip learns that Biddy proposes to leave the forge to teach in a new school in the village, that Orlick still lurks in the neighbourhood and that Joe misses him very much while saying little about it. He declares to Biddy that he will henceforth visit the forge more often and is offended when she seems dubious and insists on calling him 'Mr Pip'. After saying goodbye next morning, first to Joe at the forge and then to Biddy at the kitchen door, he sets off as the mist clears – to reveal perhaps the emptiness of his promise.

others . . . should be softened Estella.

Chapter 36

While the financial positions of the two young men further
deteriorate, the approach of Pip's twenty-first birthday arouses
anticipations. Inviting Pip on the day to his office, his guardian
greets him for the first time as 'Mr Pip' and proceeds with the
usual catechism. In spite of the recent performance with his
accounts Pip can give no exact figure for his expenses, but
admits he is in debt. He is then handed a bank note for five
hundred pounds which sum is to be his annual income, payable
quarterly, until the appearance of his benefactor in person; he
fails to get any idea of when that may be; he is merely told that
with it the lawyer's task as agent will be accomplished.

Pip invites Jaggers to dinner and, while waiting to accompany
him to Barnard's Inn, asks Wemmick's opinion on his intention
to supply enough money to establish Herbert in business, only to
receive a drastic form of warning that he will be throwing good
money away. However, this turns out to be only office advice,
that at the Walworth home may well be different.

Jaggers's suspicious manner at the dinner leaves Pip melan-
choly and Herbert with a guilty sense of having committed some
crime.

a folded piece of tissue-paper This turns up again as a bank note.
tightened his post-office Closed his mouth.

Chapter 37

The following Sunday Pip arrives at the 'Castle' in Walworth, to
find the Aged Parent alone, so conversation is one-sided until
the approach of Wemmick and a Miss Skiffins, a frequent
visitor, is announced by mechanically worked flaps bearing their
names, a device for the benefit of the deaf old man. Taking a
walk in the garden Pip unfolds to Wemmick the story of his
friendship with Herbert and his desire to repay the latter for his
help socially during the first days in London. He wishes to
provide Herbert with an income that could lead to a partnership. Wemmick, true to Walworth tradition, encourages
instead of discourages and promises to make enquiries.

They return to what is a regular Sunday meal of tea and toast in large amounts. Another custom is observed when the Aged Parent is given the newspaper from which to read aloud. During this hazardous recital Wemmick periodically steals an arm round Miss Skiffins and is gently rebuffed. At length a hot drink is produced and Pip discreetly leaves for home. After repeated visits to Wemmick there and in London a broker is found requiring a partner, and secret articles on Herbert's behalf, as negotiated by the brother of Miss Skiffins, an accountant, are signed. Pip contributes half his bank note. Herbert's delight in telling Pip his good news sends our hero to bed with tears of pleasure that he has at last made some good use of his Expectations.

Wine-Coopering Making wine barrels.
jorum A large drinking-vessel.

Chapter 38

This chapter is devoted to Pip's relations with Estella, an unhappy period of emotional torment created by an extraordinary scheme of revenge for slighted love. It is to end with the shock of an even more extraordinary scheme – a rich reward for a childhood act of sympathy. The cruel tantalizing role played to order by the daughter is to be succeeded by the still more cruel revelation that Pip's present status in society has been funded by her convict father.

As Estella's escort Pip attends a great variety of social occasions at which she attracts numerous admirers; his constant presence causes them to be jealous while he gets little satisfaction from the supposition that she is destined for him, not of her own choice but as arranged by Miss Havisham. On one occasion she shows sympathetic understanding by warning him against becoming fatally attracted by her.

Pip gives a grim account of one of their periodic visits to Satis House, marked by the only quarrel he has ever witnessed between the love-hungry old lady and the hard-hearted beauty she has done so much to create. Estella's ruthless logic brings Miss Havisham to the depths of despair and Pip takes a walk round the familiar grounds, returning to find the two reconciled. After some games of cards with Estella Pip retires for the night to another building but cannot sleep, haunted by visions of

Miss Havisham; getting up and entering the main house he catches glimpses of her real self flitting back and forth with a candle in her hand.

At a meeting of the Finches' Club, Bentley Drummle, that most unpleasant of Estella's admirers, proposes a toast to her and is challenged to a duel by Pip. The affair, however, is settled according to club rules by Drummle producing a written declaration by Estella that she has danced with him. After she has tolerated Drummle's attentions at a Richmond ball Pip rallies her about being associated with such a boor, indeed showing him more favours than she shows to Pip. Her significant parting remark that night is that her intention may be to entrap others but not him.

a perversion of ingenuity A wicked trick to make him suffer pangs of jealousy in spite of the ultimate reward being assured.
sconces Bracket candle-sticks fixed to walls.
addle-headed Stupid, from a word for a rotten egg.

Chapter 39

The *transition* from the previous chapter to this one takes the form of a fable of a stone slab long fashioned and positioned to fall by a stroke of his own hand on a sultan in the hour of victory.

Pip and Herbert are now living in the Temple, the former pursuing a course of reading, the latter progressing in the world of commerce. One evening when Herbert is absent and the weather is atrocious, the wind extinguishing lamps and the rain beating on windows, Pip hears at the late hour of eleven footsteps on the stairs and a grey-headed man emerges from the darkness with a welcoming gesture to which Pip responds with a cold request for an explanation. The stranger sits down in a chair and asks if anyone is about. When he says 'I'm glad you've grow'd up a game one' Pip recollects with disgust his meeting in the marshes with the convict. Endeavouring to make his visitor understand that circumstances have changed he offers him a drink 'before you go', but the sight of tears in the old man's eyes leads him to relent and apologize. Told of the fortune made far away in Australia, Pip asks about the mysterious messenger with the two pound notes but the ex-convict denies any knowledge of him; when Pip offers him two pound notes he quietly burns them to ashes and in his turn enquires how Pip has fared.

By referring to one fact after another the gaunt figure standing by the fire brings home to Pip who his benefactor really is and his young beneficiary faints in his arms. Proudly claiming that he has made a gentleman of Pip he admires the clothes, the jewellery, the shelves of books he has paid for; Pip himself has grown so handsome there must be a girl somewhere (a striking piece of dramatic irony). Pip is to have whatever money can buy with the wealth accumulated by so much hard labour and dedicated to this end. The ex-convict has found constant encouragement in the thought of 'possessing' a gentleman back in England.

On top of this bitter revelation Pip learns that the desire to see his creation has led his benefactor to risk his life as a returned convict. Pip takes due precautions and puts him to bed in Herbert's room and then sits down to reflect on all the implications. Recollections flood in upon his mind; remembering the actions of the man in the marshes, he quietly locks the door on the sleeping fugitive from justice.

original relations As tutor and student.
the eastward churches Wren's steeples lie east of the Temple.

Revision questions on the Second Stage

1 Describe the relationship between Pip and Herbert.

2 How many characters in these chapters turn up unexpectedly and on what occasions?

3 With how many aspects of London does Pip become familiar?

4 Trace the changes in Estella's attitude to Pip.

5 What part is played in these chapters by money affairs?

6 How many houses does Pip visit in this part of the story and for what reasons?

7 Mention three occasions when Pip's 'expectations' are referred to.

Assignments

1 Write about friendship or love in any novel you are studying.

2 How important is location or setting in your chosen book?

3 Show how the past influences the present in a book you have read.

Chapter 40

Pip passes five anxious days until the arrival of Herbert. In the darkness of the early morning he had stumbled over a figure crouching on the staircase and the watchman's reference, when questioned, to a second person renders him still more uneasy. He explains to his laundress that an 'uncle' has suddenly appeared. At breakfast the latter tells Pip his name, assumed in this country of 'Provis' and his real one, Abel Magwitch. Provis makes a hearty meal and lights an old pipe. Holding Pip's hands he expresses his admiration for his creation and then passes him a wallet full of notes to spend 'like a gentleman'.

After a sudden curse on all elements of society involved in the imposition of his prison sentence he apologizes to Pip profusely. He seeks to assure Pip that the danger of detection is less than he fears. Meanwhile the pleasure of seeing his 'gentleman' is worth the risk of being hanged. Pip finds a nearby upstairs flat, orders some articles of clothing from various shops with which to help disguise the ex-convict and calls on Jaggers who, in his non-committal way, avoids admitting any knowledge of Magwitch's movements while confirming the identity of Pip's benefactor (whom he has warned against breaking the law by returning to England from New South Wales). In this short period of close association with a man whose criminal career is stamped on every detail of his daily existence, Pip is withheld from fleeing only by the thought of Herbert. His friend is surprised to encounter such an unexpected guest especially when requested to swear on a little black testament not to give away any information to anyone.

dram A small draught of spirits.
nameless visitor Both Pip and the reader have yet to learn the ex-convict's name.
perceptibly Evidently.

prolix Involved.
blood-'uns Pedigree horses.
the Calendar The Newgate Calendar was a list of crimes.
The imaginary student Frankenstein, who, in the story by Mary Shelley, published in 1818, galvanized a soulless monster made out of human fragments in the dissecting-room.

Chapter 41

Pip sees his own fear and repugnance reflected in the expression on Herbert's face. After seeing Provis safely into his new quarters at midnight, Pip returns to share his dismay with Herbert who is proving a real friend in need. Pip tells him he has decided to decline further 'gentlemanly' expenditure and to meet his considerable debts somehow himself. Faint as this hope seems, the greater cause for concern is that Provis's probable reaction to such a rebuff will be to give himself up. As Herbert suggests, the only solution is to get Provis out of England and in order to succeed Pip will have to accompany him and contrive to escape later on.

Next morning when Provis comes round with plans for more fashionable accommodation, Pip asks him to reveal more of his past life; he does so after reminding both of them of their commitment to secrecy and his account takes up the next chapter.

in a barrack way As if confined to a barracks (or a prison).
raving off By-passing with mere talk.

Chapter 42

Provis first summarizes his life as 'in and out of jail', knowing little of his origins but somehow retaining the name of Abel Magwitch. As a vagrant child he had been continually locked up, punished and subjected to attempts at reforming his character. After years of casual labour in a variety of occupations, he had met a well-educated man called Compeyson and become his partner in forgery. Another associate had been known as 'Arthur', whom Provis saw die of delirium after visions of a woman in white chasing him with a death shroud. Thereafter Compeyson had planned the crimes which Provis had committed, thereby placing him at his mercy.

When the two had been tried in court, with separate defences, Provis's sentence was twice as long (fourteen years) on the strength of his being obviously the bad character. They both happened to be on the same convict hulk and Provis had sought his revenge by striking Compeyson, only to be consigned to the ship's black hole. Thence he had escaped to the shore where he had met Pip and then, by seizing Compeyson, also on the run, had found himself re-arrested and given a life sentence.

In a note written and handed to Pip Herbert explains that Miss Havisham's brother was called Arthur and that Compeyson was the false lover who abandoned her at the wedding.

key-metal Turning in prison locks.
My Missis Magwitch's wife is featured in a later episode.
Bridewells The Bridewell in London began as a palace and ended as a 'house of correction' for vagrants.

Chapter 43

Pip realizes the danger of Provis being detected by Compeyson who is mortally afraid of him. He decides he must see Estella (gone from Richmond to Satis House) before going abroad and pretends to Provis he is visiting Joe. At the Blue Boar he encounters Drummle; while standing before the inn fire both indulge in a shoving match and spar at each other in a scrappy conversation. Neither yields until displaced from the warm spot by three farmers.

Pip sees Drummle ride off to a dinner appointment with a lady after a word with a man 'in a dust-coloured dress' (like the mystery man at Bernard's Inn in Chapter 40) who reminds Pip of Orlick. Then he sets out for Satis.

box Boxed-in seat.

Chapter 44

Pip tells Miss Havisham and Estella what he senses they know already, that he has discovered who is his patron. Miss Havisham denies that Jaggers, by a coincidence lawyer for both herself and this patron, has been responsible for Pip's delusion and angrily rejects his accusation that she has played a trick on him. Pip, after pointing out that Matthew Pocket's family are very different from her other greedy relations, asks her to do Herbert a service (by continuing the subsidy he can no longer afford).

Pip then declares his love for Estella over the years – now that he realizes she was not intended for him after all and that he is no longer a gentleman of means. In reply Estella reminds him that love has no real meaning for one like herself without a heart; she admits seeing a lot of Drummle and finally informs him they are to be married. When Pip appeals to her not to be the instrument of Miss Havisham's revenge on the male sex, she firmly states that this is of her own free will. Seeking a change of life and against the advice of Miss Havisham, she prefers to bestow her hollow affection on a brute rather than on one more sensitive who would suffer from such a marriage. Pip draws a passionate picture of what his undying love for her has meant in the past and will do in the future, kisses her hand and walks out of Satis to go on foot distractedly the whole way back to central London.

The porter at the gate in the Temple hands him a note with the warning: 'Don't go home.' The handwriting is Wemmick's.

enrich Hardly the metaphor for the recipient of some large sums of money.

Chapter 45

Pip finds a cheap bed for the night but gets little sleep studying his dingy surroundings and worrying over the warning which usurps first place in his mind over his recollections of the visit that day to Satis House. He leaves early for Walworth and finds Wemmick at breakfast. In a cautious, 'extra-official' manner the kind-hearted clerk conveys the bare information that Magwitch's departure from Australia has been noticed and that Pip's rooms in the Temple have been watched. Asked if Compeyson is still alive he nods. Then he describes his trip to Herbert's office and gives the reasons for their decision to remove Provis to the home of Herbert's Clara, adding that Herbert has taken the old man there, leaving word at the Temple pretending that he has gone to Dover.

Wemmick suggests that Pip should go to Clara's at night;

before leaving for his work at Jaggers's office he sees Pip settled down for a day with the Aged Parent.

Divinely Righteous Arrogant. From the Stuart doctrine of the 'divine right' of kings.
Argus A hundred-eyed watchman in Greek mythology.
staring rounds The circular reflections on the wall of the holes in the lamp.
a certain part of the world Australia.
portable property Magwitch's wallet of notes.

Chapter 46

After frequently losing his way in the strange underworld of the riverside Pip eventually reaches the house in Chinks's Basin, kept by a kindly Mrs Whimple. Herbert explains that Clara's bedridden father upstairs, an ex-ship's purser who doles out the household provisions from his room, is addicted to rum; the loud thumpings on the ceiling are his summonses for attendance, in strong contrast with the quiet in the flat above him in which Provis, known here as a 'Mr Campbell', awaits further developments. Pip explains to him the dangerous circumstances, excepting Compeyson's continued existence, and broaches the plan to take him abroad. Herbert suggests they take up rowing again.

That night the precincts of the Temple are quite deserted as they return separately. Next day Pip obtains a boat and, alone or with Herbert, makes several expeditions from Temple Stairs, going beyond London Bridge and its risky arches as far as Provis's hide-out.

To Herbert the ebb-tide at night is flowing past the Temple down to his beloved; to Pip it flows down to his erstwhile benefactor (and father of *his* beloved) perhaps carrying his pursuers thither.

bow-window A bay (projecting) window which is curved like a bow.
how mild Ironic.

Chapter 47

Some weeks of tension are passed waiting for a sign from Wemmick. While embarrassed by a shortage of money since the return of the wallet to Magwitch and gloomily expecting news of

Estella's marriage, Pip is chiefly concerned over the danger of the returned convict being discovered. This chapter describes the first of two chance meetings. On a February afternoon, after his routine row down river and back, Pip dines at a local chophouse and goes on to the theatre in which he has noticed that Wopsle is playing strange parts in some light entertainment. After the performance, having observed Wopsle watching him curiously from the stage he meets the actor who informs him that someone has been sitting behind him in the audience looking very like the second convict recaptured on the marshes all those years ago. Suspecting that this may be Compeyson Pip agrees with Herbert to redouble their precautions; a letter is sent to Wemmick.

maps of the world Projected in circular frames these would be
  suggested by the series of round stains.
starlings Projections from a bridge at water level to protect it against
  the force of the current.
trousers The traditional flared bell-bottoms.
at the last Census A playful reference to the number of actors actually
  on the stage.
Swab Clumsy fellow (naval slang).

Chapter 48

The second meeting also follows a trip on the river: Pip is overtaken in Cheapside by Jaggers who invites him to dinner. After a visit to the office they go to the lawyer's house with Wemmick, who in his official capacity avoids looking at Pip but hands him a letter from Miss Havisham asking him to go and see her. Jaggers, rather insensitively, weighs the chances of Estella or Drummle gaining the mastery in marriage; when the housekeeper serves the dinner Pip observes the intentness of her look and the working of her fingers like someone knitting; he is startlingly reminded of Estella whom he promptly concludes must be her daughter.

On their way home from dinner Wemmick, questioned by Pip, reveals as much as he can of this gypsy-like woman whom Jaggers had years before cleverly defended against a charge of murdering another woman she suspected of having an affair with the tramp to whom she had been 'married'. In court the strength of the woman's wrists (see Chapter 26) had been disguised and the scratches on the victim passed off as the marks of brambles and not fingernails. The prosecution had alleged that the woman had at the same time destroyed her daughter of three years. She had been tamed by serving ever since the trial as Jaggers's housekeeper.

winding sheet The unused wax (cf. the 'snuff' in Chapter 6).
not alone With Estella (Chapter 33).
identification in the theatre Of Compeyson by Wopsle (Chapter 47).
sat under counsel Advised the barrister acting as counsel for the defence (something a solicitor could not do).
over the broomstick Illegally.

Chapter 49

Alighting at Halfway House Pip walks to the town (now identified by the cathedral as Rochester) and finds Miss Havisham greatly changed with a guilty sense of the harm done by her. She wishes to demonstrate the change by fulfilling the promise to help Herbert. The sum required is nine hundred pounds and Pip in return is to keep her secret. Her offer to give Pip himself some assistance is gently but firmly declined. First she gives him an order for the money to be disbursed by Jaggers and then kneels before him pleading for forgiveness and crying repeatedly 'What have I done?'. Pip points out the greater harm was done in deliberately turning Estella into a heartless woman and lets her know he is aware of events in her tragic life. Of Estella's origins she can tell him only that she was brought as an orphan of three by Jaggers and given her name at that time.

Before returning Pip revisits the scenes of his earlier experiences. The recurrence of a boyhood vision of Miss Havisham hanging from a beam impels him to return upstairs to make sure she is all right. On the threshold of her room he sees her run towards him in flames caught from the fire in front of which she has been kneeling. Throwing his coat and the tablecloth over her he extinguishes the flames after a fierce struggle. Servants lift her insensible body on to the table where she is attended by a surgeon; only then does Pip realize that both his hands have suffered. He leaves early next morning with Miss Havisham still pleading in semi-consciousness for him to forgive her – he does so in a parting kiss.

the old monks Among the successive revelations in the closing chapters of the novel is this first topographical indication that the town so often visited in earlier episodes is Rochester. The monks had replaced the secular canons in the eleventh century; their 'nooks of ruin' are mostly in the *deanery* garden, so-called after the Dissolution when the Prior was replaced under the New Foundation by a Dean.

a new desolation The permanent absence of Estella.
a looking-glass A reflection of her own early love.

Chapter 50

Suffering in mind and body Pip is tenderly nursed by Herbert; a speedy recovery of his hands is essential to further rowing. Herbert, who has been visiting Clara and spent two hours in conversation with the fugitive upstairs, gives Pip Provis's account of his relationship with the wild woman, Jaggers's housekeeper. She had threatened to destroy their child and actually disappeared with it after the trial for murder at which she had been acquitted, thanks to Jaggers. Magwitch, reluctant to give any evidence against the woman he had lived with, had kept away from the court. Compeyson had known of this abstention and had used it to force further criminal deeds upon him.

When Pip asks whether any date was mentioned Herbert calculates that all this must have happened about four years before the encounter in the churchyard where, so Provis told him, Pip made him think of the daughter he had lost and who would have been the same age. The excited Pip then declares that Provis down-river must be Estella's father.

some woman Molly, whose story is avoided by Magwitch in Chapter 42 and told by Wemmick in Chapter 48.

Chapter 51

In his impatience to get confirmation of his belief Pip visits Jaggers and, after a more detailed account of his injuries, produces the order for the money for Herbert which prompts the lawyer to express regret that Pip himself is to get no benefit. He then explains that he has been told all Miss Havisham knows about Estella and adds that he is now even better informed. He tells the staggered but unruffled Jaggers that he knows who Estella's mother and father are. In the face of this revelation of secrets that he has personally harboured Jaggers turns to Wemmick for a resumption of their work on the accounts.

Pip therefore makes a passionate appeal to Jaggers for greater confidence in one who has been so emotionally involved and, not succeeding, switches to Wemmick, mentioning the latter's pleasant home with his old father which has been taboo in the office. This incidental discovery leads to a more human understanding between lawyer and clerk; Jaggers goes on to 'put a case' without making any 'concessions'. From this the reader gathers that, anxious to save a pretty child from juvenile crime and consulted over a child to be adopted, Jaggers had taken the girl from her mother as a condition of his acting for her in the law-court and offered her for adoption. Bringing the 'case' up-to-date he then demands to know who will benefit from the secret of Estella's parentage becoming known – better that Pip should have both his hands chopped off!

Silence being generally consented to, Pip watches the two 'professionals' resume their accounting and revert to their former mutual inflexibility. This return to normal is emphasized by the farcical ejection from the office of a wretched regular client who has offended by introducing 'feelings' in the shape of a tear – over a *daughter* in trouble with the law!

an indefinably attentive stop A pause during which he is paying close attention for reasons not yet clear.
the usual performance See Chapter 29.
unposted his pen Taken it out of his mouth.

Chapter 52

Pip completes his one good deed by securing Herbert's partnership in Clarriker's, though the prospect of his friend's managing a new branch in the East threatens a further separation. A message from Wemmick suggests the departure of Provis on the following Wednesday; as Pip is still incapacitated they think of enlisting Startop. Once they get Provis on board an outward-bound steamer Pip would go with him. They decide on a Hamburg steamer, Pip sees to passports, Herbert obtains the aid of Startop and all other matters are agreed.

An anonymous note is delivered, challenging Pip to come alone and in secret to a place in the marshes for information about his 'uncle' Provis. Leaving a note to Herbert he is just in time to catch the coach. Putting up at an inn he is angered by the landlord's conversation at dinner informing him of a local young man's ingratitude to his chief benefactor, Pumblechook! Humbled by this indirect rebuke for his neglect of Joe and Biddy, Pip leaves for his appointment with the unknown at nine.

stick to his pepper and rum Die from excessive drinking.
like a font Some medieval fonts had octagonal covers but this apartment may have been a chapterhouse.

Chapter 53

Pip makes his way in the darkness across the marshes to the designated limekiln. Seeing a lighted candle inside he enters and calls out. As he takes up the candle he is lassoed and tied up to a ladder near the wall. When his assailant relights the candle Pip recognizes Orlick, who threatens to make him pay for getting him dismissed from the forge. The sacked journeyman and ex-gatekeeper at Satis declares Pip has always been his 'enemy'; he goes on to say that he is going to remove him 'out of his way' and destroy all traces by burning his body in the limekiln. In desperation Pip envisages all the misunderstandings among his friends that will arise from his disappearance; Orlick, however, takes time to gloat drunkenly over his captive. He boasts of his attack on Mrs Joe and blames it on Pip as the boy had been given better treatment.

In this critical situation images from the past flash through Pip's mind. He learns next that Orlick had been the figure crouching on the stairs at the Temple and the other figure following on the heels of Provis. Orlick has also been in contact with Compeyson (the forger writes letters for him). As he picks up a sledge-hammer to finish off his victim the latter shouts and struggles against his bonds, at which point rescuing figures force their way in and grapple with Orlick, who escapes and vanishes into the dark. Pip recovers consciousness to see first the face of Trabb's Boy, then those of Herbert, supporting him, and Startop. He learns that the time for Provis's departure has not passed by and he is escorted across the marshes to return immediately to the Temple which they reach next morning. On the way Pip is told how he came to be rescued; finding Orlick's note on the floor and suspecting trouble, Herbert, with Startop, had taken a fast coach to the Blue Boar whence, guided by Trabb's Boy who had observed Pip's movements, they had reached the limekiln and at once heard Pip's cries for help. Pip spends the next day in bed worrying about their scheme for Provis and grows nearly delirious over the possibility of his being unfit to take part.

Early next morning, however, he is up before the others; they watch for the incoming tide to turn.

a gun with a brass-bound stock See Chapter 29.
my words to Biddy See Chapter 35.
wolf This puzzling appellation may indicate that Orlick regards Pip as a hostile animal to be destroyed or as a creature that seizes what belongs to others.
weazen Throat; Caliban's word in *The Tempest* is 'wezand', 3,2.
the popular local version Pumblechook's. See the last chapter.
disappointment This exaggeration is probably due to Pip's earlier encounter with this lively customer.

Chapter 54

The three young men set off from Temple Stairs in their boat at high water, hoping to reach a quiet part of the river below Gravesend where Pip and Provis will be able to board one of two steamers whose departure from London they have ascertained to be at nine next morning. Rowing past both these vessels they approach Mill Pond Bank and, seeing no suspicious signs, take Provis into the boat dressed like a river-pilot. The old man is the least anxious of the party and talks to Pip of their future together in a foreign country. They continue down river until dark when they land at a lonely inn which, while not too clean, does provide food and drink as well as safe lodging. Nevertheless they are made apprehensive when they hear from the landlord's man about a galley hovering in the neighbourhood which is suspected of being manned by customs officers. Rising during the night Pip observes two men examining their boat and then crossing the marsh.

In the morning Pip suggests that he and Provis should be picked up at a more distant spot. There, having ensured that no one is about, they await the boat which duly arrives to take them out into the track of the steamers. As both vessels come round the bend and the two intending travellers are saying farewell to their friends, a galley joins them in mid-stream. When the Hamburg paddle-steamer has come close to them a voice from the galley names the returned convict and demands his immediate surrender. Both boats are suddenly locked together in the path of the steamer but, before his boat is run down, Pip sees Magwitch unmask a muffled figure in the galley whom he recognizes as Compeyson. When he is rescued from the water Pip watches Magwitch swim back after his enemy has disappeared as they both have fallen overboard. After the search for Compeyson has been abandoned the party assembles in the inn. Provis, who has injuries to head and chest, tells Pip that he merely freed himself from the other's grasp. When he comes to change into dry clothes his wallet (the balance of Pip's 'great expectations') is confiscated.

Pip stays with Magwitch on his return to London and prison where the latter is certain to receive a severe sentence. Pip is now devoted to one whom he had at first shunned – now that his expectations have come to nothing. Magwitch, however, is quite content to have seen *his* boy grown into a gentleman. Holding his hand Pip vows to stay by his side as long as he is allowed to.

pea-coats Otherwise pea-jackets, short woollen coats worn by sailors.
coal-whippers Men who raised coal out of the holds by means of pulleys.
respondent Answering back.
fenders Coils of rope hung over a ship's side to prevent damage by collision.
troubled waters Cloudy water from stirred-up mud in contrast with 'clearer river'.
thowels Rowlocks.
Jack Serving-man.
rattling Having violent effects.
the Nore Lightship on a sandbank off the River Medway marking the mouth of the Thames.

Chapter 55

The trial of Magwitch is delayed three days for identification of the returned convict by a former officer of the prison-ship. Jaggers is annoyed at Pip's allowing the money to be so easily confiscated while Magwitch is satisfied that Pip's inheritance is safe in the lawyer's hands. During the month that is to elapse before the trial Herbert 'breaks the news' to *his* benefactor that he is being posted to the branch in Cairo; then he brings up the question of Pip's future with the information that a clerk may be needed out there, adding that Clara would warmly welcome a third member of their future household.

After seeing Herbert off on his sea-voyage Pip returns to the Temple and meets Wemmick on the stairs. The clerk explains that his unlucky choice of a day for the attempted escape had been made on the false assumption that Compeyson was away somewhere. Wemmick is even more grieved over the loss of so much 'portable property' which could have been saved whereas its owner could not.

As Wemmick is taking a most unusual holiday, he begs Pip to come to Walworth the following Monday to go on a walk with him. The surprise of all Walworth surprises is an accidentally contrived wedding, at a conveniently discovered church, of Wemmick to Miss Skiffins, given away by the Aged Parent. After endeavouring to be the life and soul of this odd wedding breakfast Pip wishes his friend joy and promises this time to betray no more Walworth sentiments in Little Britain.

never mistrusted but Never believed other than.
exordium Introductory remarks.
Hymen Classical god of marriage, the double meaning of 'sacrifice' is the agony of getting his gloves on.

Chapter 56

Lying seriously injured in the prison infirmary Magwitch is visited daily by Pip who watches him grow steadily weaker without his ever complaining. He seems to find solace in the thought that his desperate character is now changed for the better, a transformation begun so long ago in the churchyard.

In court Pip is able to hold his hand as he sits in the dock; the inevitable sentence of death is passed on him together with thirty-one others. Pip vividly recollects the sentencing of this whole group and the judge's address which singles out Magwitch's career of crime for particular reference. Magwitch briefly acknowledges a lesser sentence than that already received from God.

Pip spends days penning appeals to every authority he thinks capable of showing mercy; among his worst recollections of London are its street scenes during his desperate haunting of the offices where his petitions have been lodged. The officers carry out their duties with due care for a dying prisoner. On the tenth day after sentence Pip finds Magwitch weak but uncomplaining and grateful for Pip's constant attendance. As he holds his boy's hand close to his heart the Governor appears to give Pip permission to stay beyond the allotted time and to speak in privacy. For some reason Pip has delayed till this moment to tell Magwitch that he has a beautiful daughter and that he, Pip, loves her. Raising Pip's hand to his lips the ex-convict passes quietly away.

the singleness of my designs My having one purpose and one only.
more comfortable Less conscious of the criminal connection.
the two men ... the Temple to pray See St Luke xviii,9–14.

Chapter 57

Hard pressed financially, Pip gives notice to terminate his tenancy of the rooms in the Temple; he grows progressively weaker and more listless. One morning, waking from a nightmare of disconnected scenes based on his past experiences, he finds himself arrested for debt but the bailiffs, seeing his condition, withdraw. Then follow a number of strange hallucinations before he becomes aware of being nursed instead of assaulted; the variety of faces belonging to those attending to him settle down into the countenance of – Joe.

At length, mustering courage, he asks this constant companion if it really is Joe and gets the familiar reply: 'which dear old Pip, old chap, you and me was ever friends.' Pip learns that Joe had come at once, urged by Biddy; he watches him perform laboriously the task of writing a *letter* to Biddy on the result of his efforts (a feat now rendered possible by Biddy's teaching). Then he is given such news as Joe can convey: Miss Havisham has left in her will a substantial sum to Matthew Pocket and mere pittances to the other relatives; Orlick has been jailed for his part in a robbery with violence carried out on Pumblechook. During Pip's slow recovery Joe looks after him with great tenderness and the same honest simplicity of earlier days so that the invalid imagines he is a boy again and that all that has intervened is a bad dream. The joy of the first drive in midsummer into the country on a Sunday with the church bells ringing is such that, overcome with emotion, he lays his head on Joe's shoulder.

The same evening, when asked by Pip what he knows of his 'patron' Joe hedges in his replies and suggests leaving some past topics alone as irrelevant. Instead he explains how he had been prevented from saving Pip from his sister's canings by the fear of worse to follow. Pip notices that as he himself grows stronger Joe becomes more uneasy and even addresses him as 'sir'. Pip is reluctant to let him know of his impecunious state; then one Monday morning he finds that Joe has gone back to the forge overnight, having paid the debt for which Pip had faced arrest. He decides to follow him with a sorrowful apology and, 'secondly', make a proposal of marriage to Biddy. He rehearses this proposal carefully beforehand.

orthographical stumbling-block Problem of spelling.
coddleshell Joe's pronunciation of 'codicil'.
conventional temperature 'Cool' was already a conventional epithet to emphasize a large sum of money.

Chapter 58

Having arrived at the Blue Boar, Pip is given inferior accommodation on account of his change of fortune. He calls at Satis before breakfast and finds the house is due to be pulled down and the furniture up for sale. Pumblechook is at the inn, condescending in his pretended sympathy and even presiding in his usual fashion over Pip's breakfast; his odious hypocrisy is such that Pip angrily orders him to take his hands off the teapot. This merely leads to a further and even more preposterous suggestion that Pip should tell Joe of his having just seen his 'earliest benefactor' and to the repeated charge of ingratitude. Pumblechook hastily departs to continue his harangue to a local audience outside his shop.

In perfect weather Pip approaches the forge, buoyed up by prospects of a future life in his old home. Biddy's school and the forge are both closed and he comes upon Joe and Biddy arm in arm – just married. At first overcome by this surprise, Pip manages to share their joy, thanks them for all their past kindnesses and informs them that he is about to go abroad to earn the money needed to repay Joe for settling his debts. He pictures another little Pip in the chimney corner and begs their forgiveness. He then asks to be allowed to revisit his old room and, after a meal together, to be accompanied on his way as far as the finger-post.

In two months' time Pip is a clerk in Cairo and shortly after that is left in charge when Herbert returns to England to marry

Clara. Having spent several years living a pleasant existence with Herbert and Clara, paying off his debts and corresponding with Joe and Biddy, he is made a partner. Eventually the secret of his benefaction is revealed to Herbert and this just adds to their happiness. The firm's modest but steady success owes much to Herbert's ability which went unsuspected by Pip in their early days together.

in charity and love with all mankind Echoing the Communion Service 'in love and charity with your neighbours'.

Chapter 59

After eleven years Pip returns to England and, visiting the forge, finds a new edition of himself in the chimney corner. He takes the boy to the churchyard and sits him on the tombstone of dreaded memory (yet associated with Magwitch). When Biddy tactfully enquires about Estella he professes to have got over that dream; nevertheless he decides to revisit the ruins of Satis for the sake of the woman he still loves, now a widow after a ruinous existence with her brute of a husband.

He reaches the site in the gathering dusk; having traced the remains of various buildings he sees a figure in the garden walk. He is amazed to find it is Estella – they have both come back to the place for the first time after leaving it. He is told that the ground is still hers by inheritance, the last item in her possession; she is paying it a last visit before it is built on and so changed in appearance. After asking about his life abroad she admits having thought often about him and then, recalling their previous separation, begs that they remain friends – apart.

They leave hand in hand; writing his story years afterwards and leaving the reader in ignorance whether he is single or married Pip merely adds the enigmatic remark: 'I saw no shadow of another parting from her.'

the placid look Magwitch's, when dying.
the last words Telling him of Estella.
since my duty has not been incompatible ... remembrance Does this rather obscure allusion imply that the task imposed on her as a ward of avenging Miss Havisham on the male sex does not preclude cherishing the recollection of his affection?

Revision questions on the Third Stage

1 Tell the story of Pip's whole connection with Miss Havisham.

2 What facts from the hidden past are revealed at this stage?

3 Describe the plans for Magwitch's escape and explain their failure.

4 Pip's two greatest friends save his life on different occasions. Give an account in each case.

5 Tell the story of Pip in these last chapters as (a) Joe, (b) Herbert might have related it.

6 What is added to this novel by the background of (a) the River Thames (b) mists?

Assignments

1 Write about an exciting escape or attempt to escape in any book you have read.

2 How important is a secret or secrets to the plot of your chosen book?

3 Write about any scene or incident in a novel you have studied which is profoundly sad.

4 Give an account of any character in a novel you have read whose feelings are changed as a result of experience.

5 Write a summary of the ending of a book you have studied which is neither happy nor unhappy.

Charles Dickens's art in *Great Expectations*
Characters

With each new novel Dickens added a set of characters to his gallery of studies of men and women unexcelled for their vitality and variety. Often their very abundance was out of all proportion to the story, but by the time he came to write *Great Expectations* he had managed to strike a closer balance between plot and characters. There is, too, a clearly drawn contrast between the simple, honest, patient and faithful folk on the one hand and the proud, avaricious, spiteful and hypocritical on the other.

Dickens had a unique gift for portraying two types: the outcast and the eccentric, here represented by Magwitch and Miss Havisham. These two, actuated by very different kinds of revenge, create between them all the complications necessary for a highly involved, though well-knit plot; a third character, the hidden villain, Compeyson, is the prime mover, since prior to the events of the story, his wickedness drove the other two to make their respective plans. Compeyson is also the ultimate instrument of fate in compassing the arrest of Magwitch and indirectly the disappearance of Pip's fortune.

The formidable lawyer, Jaggers, and his efficient clerk, Wemmick, are 'agents', carrying out the wishes of others with the utmost discretion and a complete lack of feeling (except in Walworth); Orlick, that creeping spirit of the marshes, is the agent of everything evil; the self-effacing Joe and the shrewd, placid Biddy represent the good influences of a happy and contented, if humble, home life; Herbert is a true friend to Pip, sharing his plans, rescuing him in the nick of time and enabling him in the end to make good; his successful partnership and the bequest to his father are both conferred by Miss Havisham through the influence of Pip whose own expectations ultimately come to nothing. As Estella points out, she and Pip are really puppets, yet each makes a vital decision against his or her own interests: he deliberately refuses to accept his fortune when he knows from whom it comes; she deliberately marries a brute to spare Pip a loveless marriage.

The remaining characters are of minor importance, yet the least significant among them does not escape without some distinguishing mark by which to be remembered. Dickens believed passionately in the men and women he created and a wide range of experience in reporting as well as his concentrated and accurate gift of observation furnished him with ample materials. Scattered through the book are vignettes from the life of tavern landlords, lodging-house landladies, waiters, coachmen, warders, shopkeepers and boy assistants.

With all his characters, great and small, Dickens had a trick of fixing them by stressing one particular feature or gesture or by the use of a special phrase: Matthew Pocket distractedly trying to lift himself by his hair, Mr Jaggers pausing at the crucial moment with his handkerchief on the way to his nose, Mr Wemmick's 'post-office of a mouth', Joe's anticipation of happy co-operation, 'What larks!' It is this device that has given rise to the criticism that Dickens saw his characters almost entirely from without, that there is little study of inner motives and emotions.

There is certainly a wealth of gesture in this book, the hands alone being given considerable significance: Jaggers biting his forefinger when he is about to squeeze admissions out of others; Magwitch holding out both hands in order to admire the gentleman he has created; Pumblechook obsequiously shaking hands; Wemmick's hand stealing round Miss Skiffin's waist; the knitting action of the fingers peculiar to both Estella and her mother Molly, the housekeeper.

It should be noted how nearly all the characters in the book undergo a change, striking or subtle. Apart from the softened mood of Magwitch and the hysterical remorse of Miss Havisham, even the imperturbable Jaggers is betrayed into a weak moment; the otherwise steady Joe oscillates between affection for Pip and respect for 'Mr Pip'; Wemmick leads a Jekyll and Hyde existence between Walworth and Little Britain; Estella develops a tenderness towards Pip as Pip does towards Magwitch. Two vicious people show no human feeling whatever, the brute Drummle and the toady, Sarah Pocket. Otherwise there is much true sympathy expressed throughout the book by a number of those who make the briefest of appearances, such as the governor of the prison and the landlady at Chinks's Basin.

Dickens's novels are remarkable for their detailed and realistic pictures of the interiors of houses and these usually have a close connection with the characters of their occupants. Besides Satis House, with its shutters, sheets and cobwebs, there is the carefully preserved parlour at the forge – used only once a year at Christmas while the rest of the house is undergoing a fierce cleaning-up at the hands of that merciless housekeeper, Mrs Joe; Pumblechook's premises, with their flavour of seeds tied up in brown paper packets in rows of little drawers. Then there is the Pocket household where the master and mistress are so preoccupied that their domestic affairs and large family are left in the charge of a large staff of servants; the 'Castle', where Wemmick brushes away the Newgate cobwebs by indulging his taste for engineering, carpentry, plumbing and gardening; Jaggers's room with its solid furniture, library of law books and papers brought home from the office; the office itself, small and dismal and dominated by the two plaster-casts of executed criminals.

Food is also given considerable significance in association with character: the 'freemasonry of Pip and Joe' over their progress in nibbling the thick slices of bread doled out to them by Mrs Gargery; the gormandizing Pumblechook keeping Pip from eating by setting him sums in mental arithmetic; the Aged Parent entrusted with preparing a 'haystack' of buttered toast; Jaggers methodically dispensing wine and sauces from his dumbwaiter; Pip entertaining Herbert with a sumptuous banquet out of his own resources and later regaling Estella on her arrival in London with a tea as bafflingly unsatisfactory as his own relationship with her; the heavy 'grubbing' of Magwitch, and Barley's huge breakfast; Miss Havisham roaming about at midnight in search of scraps. Unlike so many novelists whose characters never have time to eat, Dickens supplies some of his with complete menus!

Dickens nearly always draws attention to the eyes: Pumblechook's dull and staring; Miss Havisham's dark and flashing; Jaggers's sharp and suspicious; Wemmick's small and glittering; Biddy's thoughtful and attentive; Joe's of an undecided blue; Compeyson's shifty; Orlick's fixed on the ground; and the eye of the stranger in Chapter 10 half-shut.

Pip

The roof of my stronghold dropped upon me

Pip's self-portrait is a frank one. His recollection of the events that changed him from a humble blacksmith's boy to a young man of fashion is interspersed with reflections on his various motives in which he does not attempt to disguise his shrinking from secret terrors, his morbid fears and his mean pretences. On the other hand, even a snob is not devoid of good intentions, and Pip, while concerned to show himself the victim of circumstances, can point to the good that he has done to others. He is, indeed, with the exception of his sister and Orlick, obviously liked by the chief characters in the book. The only two objective descriptions of him come very close together (Chapter 30): one by Herbert, and rather in his favour, 'a good fellow, with impetuosity and hesitation, boldness and diffidence, action and dreaming, curiously mixed in him'; the other, a burlesque by Trabb's Boy, who mimics his bearing and exclaims, 'Pon my soul, don't know yah!' He rejects both representations!

Pip's early experience of home life is very unhappy, and only the realization that it is 'sanctified' by Joe causes him regret at leaving it. The only survivor of six infant boys, he is made by his sister to feel that his birth was a misfortune and that he would be better in his grave. Regarded by all but Joe with abhorrence as naturally 'vicious', he is given the smallest portions of food, and, worst humiliation of all, is constantly reminded by Pumblechook, 'uncle' only in name, to be grateful to 'them which brought you up by hand'. The boy has no childhood playmate and his sister's unmerciful use of 'Tickler' renders him deeply sensitive, obstinate and reticent. Pip suffers agonies of suspense, tells amazing lies and his imagination conjures up fearful ideas of what might happen to him. Early conflict with injustice, such as the confiscation of his small earnings, renders him morally timid.

Though used to country exercises, Pip has a habit of falling asleep and even of swooning, as when Magwitch reveals himself. He endures nightmares of apprehension, and lies awake at night or rises to listen at the window. He lives in constant dread of some discovery – the theft of the pie; his 'murder' of Uncle Pumblechook; his assault on Herbert. At such times everything wears an accusing air – the hare in the pantry or the cattle on the marshes. When faced by death in the hut by the limekiln, a series of visions passes rapidly through Pip's mind: everybody misconstruing his actions; his sister's illness; the murderer slouching into the village inn while his victim dissolves in vapour; his rooms at Barnard's Inn on that fatal night; the fugitive waiting in vain at Chinks's Basin. During his fever his imagination runs riot.

This is the sensitive nature that is first made conscious of being a 'common labouring boy' by the pretty girl commenting on his coarse hands and thick boots. To her teasing he owes his 'hankerings after money and gentility'. On her account particularly he shrinks from the taint of prison and crime that seems to cling to him so that he trembles at the word 'convict' – and, ironically, it is on account of a convict's daughter! When the money is mysteriously provided, seemingly for the express purpose of his acquiring the gentility necessary to find favour in Estella's eyes, his home surroundings seem 'monotonous acquaintances' compared with the life awaiting him in London. Though Pip sheds tears at the signpost, he has avoided bringing Joe with him as far as the coach. This is the beginning of a series of subterfuges, each of which leads to a feeling of shame: when he avoids Pumblechook, he runs into Trabb's Boy; when he avoids the Blue Boar on his way to meet Orlick in the marshes and stays at a smaller inn, he has to listen to the tale of his 'ingratitude' to Pumblechook – a terrible indirect rebuke for his treatment of Joe.

Pip's inheritance quickly impresses him with the power of money. The realization of his 'wild fancy' leads him to take whatever is given him (and Magwitch's provision is that he should be educated, not for a profession, but for a life of leisure) in the belief that fate destined him to be the wealthy husband of a beautiful woman. He witnesses the toadying of Miss Havisham's relatives and the toadying, to himself, of the shopkeepers. The prospect of an unlimited purse leads him into improvidence and, in the person of the Avenger, ostentation.

For Pip's mistaken belief that Miss Havisham is his benefactress, it must be said that there were significant indications in that direction. When Jaggers informs him that the name is a profound secret, he adds, 'If you have a suspicion in your own breast, keep that suspicion in your own breast'; when Pip visits Miss Havisham before his departure for London, she recalls Sarah Pocket to gloat over the discomfiture caused by Pip's 'gay figure'. He therefore tends to forget that, after rewarding him for his wheeling of her chair with twenty-five guineas towards his apprenticeship, she has said there would be nothing more. Not until much later is he to realize that it is only by a coincidence that Miss Havisham and Magwitch employed the same lawyer; but on that coincidence is built the whole fabric of his dreams.

Pip regards money merely as a means to an end. When Estella is betrothed to Drummle he has no further use for it. In his own words, nature and circumstances have made him romantic. He worships Estella from the first meeting and continues to do so 'against all reason'. Outside the gloomy walls of Satis, Estella and her guardian are associated by him with all that is picturesque and enchanting. Not even Estella's words of warning could change a passionate devotion that, all along, is obvious to Herbert. When he discovers her parentage, some of his romantic regard for her is transferred to Magwitch. On his return to England a sentimental desire to visit the garden in which he once walked with Estella brings him face to face with her, an ending which, highly artificial as it may seem, undoubtedly satisfies our sense of what is fair. His attachment to his bedroom and the village signpost is still strong when he takes leave of Joe and Biddy before going abroad.

If Pip has much for which to be forgiven by these two, he has also much to forgive in the wrong done him by Miss Havisham and, under her influence, by Estella. That he forgives both freely (even as he can remember his sister without rancour) is proof that, beneath the surface, his true nature was not spoilt by his 'Great Expectations'.

Joe Gargery

'God bless you, dear old Pip, old chap!'

This village blacksmith stands for all that is honest, respectable, proud and affectionate among the humble poor whom Dickens knew so well. He is one of nature's gentlemen, and his character sweetens the whole book, 'a mild, good-natured, sweet-tempered, easy-going, foolish, dear fellow – a sort of Hercules in strength, and also in weakness'.

Joe is never at home outside his forge. His best clothes make him resemble a respectable scarecrow and his manners in strange company are extraordinarily uncouth. He is amused at first by Pip's efforts to improve him because his simple pride in his own work rejects any thought of leaving it for any 'higher sphere'. Joe stays in London only long enough to deliver his message from Miss Havisham (a message that makes Pip ashamed of his cold welcome of the messenger) and once Pip has recovered from his fever tactfully departs for home after paying Pip's debts. The same delicate tact leads him to change the subject when Pip tries to discuss his financial predicament.

Joe sees good in everybody, even his brute of a father, and the memory of his mother makes him chivalrous to all women, even his termagant wife. He hates lies (but he deviates into fiction in order to gratify Mrs Joe with an imaginary communication of Miss Havisham's compliments). He can knock down the hulking Orlick and nurse Pip with a woman's tenderness. He warns Pip as a 'true friend' that he would never 'get to be oncommon' through crooked ways. Throughout his interview with Miss Havisham he persists in addressing his replies to Pip in a manner 'expressive of forcible argumentation, strict confidence, and great politeness', but, when badgered by Jaggers about accepting a sum of money in compensation for losing the boy's services, he adopts a pugilistic attitude which scares the lawyer, so dreaded in town, out of the room.

Joe's speech is illiterate almost to absurdity but conviction shines through it. Nothing is more forceful than a sentence begun by him with 'Which!' He admits he is 'awful dull' and regards the writing of a letter as the height of scholarship; yet, slowly raking the fire in the kitchen or smoking his pipe at the Three Jolly Bargemen, he 'beat out' for himself a philosophy and a code of conduct: 'Pip, dear old chap, life is made of ever so many partings *welded* together, as I may say.' His maxims, indeed, are of the simplest: 'manners is manners', when Pip had apparently bolted his slice of bread; 'lies is lies', when he finds Pip's glorified version of events at Satis is completely untrue; 'a gridiron *is* a gridiron', when Pip hankers after visiting Miss Havisham to thank her. To Joe, a blacksmith was a blacksmith, and at a loss away from his forge.

Mrs Gargery

'Drat that boy'

The blacksmith's wife – 'Mrs Joe' to her small brother – is one of those formidable women so frequently created by Dickens. Tall and bony and given to scrubbing everybody and everything, herself included, she regards her apron as a symbol of slavery. She has a habit of forcing herself into a passion and, when Pip is to blame, punishes her husband as well. She is an unscrupulous spy and a toady to Uncle Pumblechook. On her husband, who admires in her a 'master-mind' and a 'fine figure of a woman', she lavishes the most abusive epithets, such as 'stuck pig' and 'king of the noodles'. At times she throws things at him, Pip included. Her dustpan is the sign of her wrath, just as 'Tickler' is her instrument of punishment.

Biddy

'The best wife in the whole world'

After Mrs Joe has been disabled by a more powerful blow than any she has herself inflicted, Biddy brings to Joe and his forge a complete transformation – from constant quarrels and back-biting to steady trust and affection. Plain and unassuming in manner, Biddy has more than her share of feminine intuition. Her shrewd thrusts ruffle Pip's new-found conceit of himself more than anything else, more even than Estella's taunts. She is to become the mother of a younger Pip sitting on his stool in his old corner.

Abel Magwitch

'Yes, Pip, dear boy, I've made a gentleman of you'

It is the fate of Abel Magwitch, alias Provis, alias Mr Campbell, to be twice hunted down as a fugitive from the law into whose clutches he first fell early in life through bad company. As a boy he was known as a hardened character who spent more time in gaol than out of it. As the accomplice of Compeyson (the gentle-man turned crook) he was arrested and sentenced to fourteen years in the Hulks. Compeyson escaped with a seven-year sen-tence by getting his counsel to put most of the blame on Mag-witch, who determined to avenge himself. Having escaped from the Hulks (Chapter 1) he brings about his own recapture by going after Compeyson, who has got away about the same time, to drag him back to prison. His attempted escape results in transportation to Australia and there in a lonely shepherd's hut he thinks much of the boy who had brought him food and a file without betraying him and determines, when he inherits some property and has prospered in sheep-breeding, to turn this boy into a better gentleman than Compeyson.

If Pip has reason to feel ashamed of Joe's behaviour, he has far more reason to be disgusted by Magwitch's manners. Accustomed only to prison life or the solitudes of Australia, Magwitch, a powerful man with long iron-grey hair, eats ravenously, using his jack-knife, smokes 'negro-head' tobacco, drinks rum and water and plays Patience with a battered pack of cards. He has a peculiar click in his throat and carries a black Testament on which he not only swears oaths but keeps himself up to his own resolutions. Magwitch's one great resolve redeems his character. In the pride of his creation he finds himself but his determination to see in the flesh the 'gentleman what I made' leads to his second and final recapture. Towards the end he becomes strangely softened in manner and reconciled to his lot. In the bold bid for freedom Magwitch is the least anxious of the party. The old vengeful spirit flashes out when he seizes Compeyson and drags him under (a fitting end to such a villain). However, Magwitch stands trial with dignity and dies content in the knowledge that his 'gentleman' loves his own long-lost daughter.

Estella

'Pip, will you never take warning?'

The character of Magwitch's daughter, Miss Havisham's protégée and Pip's beloved, is not easy to delineate. She is the beautiful offspring of a criminal and a gypsy. Transferred to a rich but eccentric household at the age of three, Estella becomes Miss Havisham's creation in a far more complete sense than that in which Pip was Magwitch's. She submits to her training as a breaker of men's hearts, but when, beautiful and accomplished, she is reproached by Miss Havisham for denying her the affection this morbid woman has endeavoured to breed out of her, she calmly rebukes her 'mother by adoption' for such an unreasonable attitude.

Estella openly regards herself and Pip as puppets and behaves as though they are intended for each other but candidly warns him that her heart is devoid of 'sympathy – sentiment – nonsense'. In her flowing hair and the action of her fingers when knitting she resembles her mother – whether she ever learns who her parents are we are not told. We know only that Jaggers is against her receiving the information.

Pip cannot believe that there can be such beauty without a

heart. It enchants him from the day when he first hears her clear voice call from the window and sees her candle coming along the passage like a star, to the day of his passionate declaration of love, the last time he is to see her for eleven years. And on reflection, the reader may be justified in wondering whether Estella's 'inaccessibility' is not, after all, a pose. Estella has been allowed by Miss Havisham to go out into the 'daylight' to add elegance and refinement to her beauty and thus might possibly have learned to see human relationships in truer proportion. We know that she has been warned that love is a snare and Pip is told quite plainly that she understands such a sentiment as a mere 'form of words'; the look she gives him is one of 'incredulous wonder' when he reveals how much she has become a part of him. Yet something of the 'bent and broken' Estella who sheds silent tears in the moonlight may be glimpsed when she not only warns Pip of his intended fate at her hands but by her own act chooses to accept Drummle in order to spare the man 'who would soonest feel that I took nothing to him'. Twice Estella makes it clear to him that she differentiates between him and all others. Her self-sacrifice is a heavy one for it is not Drummle but she who is to be the victim of the marriage.

Miss Havisham

'Hear me, Pip! Love her!'

The spoilt child of a wealthy brewer; an heiress infatuated with an obvious intriguer; a bride deserted on her wedding morning; a recluse existing morbidly in a darkened house where no reckoning is kept of the passage of time – such is the strange woman who, when she has the whim to see a child play, sends for a boy from the neighbourhood. When Pip sees Miss Havisham, she reminds him of a waxwork image and a disinterred skeleton he has once seen; she resembles a witch as she hobbles about leaning on her stick with, which she is accustomed to emphasize her remarks. She gloats over the discomfiture of her jealous relatives and the beauty of the girl she has adopted and named. She urges Pip to love Estella in a tone that suggests hate rather than love.

Dickens calls her mania the 'vanity of sorrow'. By living such a solitary life she shuts out all healthy influences and suffers for it, mentally and physically. Her remorse begins when Pip unfolds his love for Estella; she holds her hand to her heart and her face assumes a ghastly look. Her death is caused by brooding over the fire until her faded bridal dress, tattered and highly inflammable, catches fire. Though she seeks to quench love in Estella, Miss Havisham yearns for it for herself and calls the girl ungrateful; in the terrible scene in which she reproaches herself – 'What have I done?' – she explains that at first she intended only to save Estella from a misery like her own. In Pip's ardent young face she sees the love she herself has once felt; in trying to save her life he suffers burns that are nothing compared with the emotional torment she has caused him.

Mr Jaggers

'I didn't say so, Mr Pip. I am putting a case'

True to his description of himself as a mere 'agent', Mr Jaggers originates nothing, evil or good, but carries out the commission of others. Before the events which happen in the book he did, indeed, choose Estella for Miss Havisham's adopted daughter (just as Pumblechook chose Pip when asked for a playmate for Estella) but thereafter he does what he is paid to do and no more.

Nevertheless, Jaggers's dominating personality gives him an aspect of fate itself. To him the human race is always in trouble, children being 'spawned' to find their way, sooner or later, into the 'net' of himself and others of his profession. He impresses all whom he meets with the idea that he knows something about them 'to their disadvantage'. Herbert is probably not the only one to come away from a conversation with him feeling that he has committed some crime. His formidable manner terrifies all with whom he comes into contact or who know him only by reputation – clerks, turnkeys, coachmen, even the judge on his bench – and he positively defies burglars to enter his premises. Jaggers bullies everybody and everything, from witnesses in court to the very sandwich he is munching. His cross-examinations extend to a chance acquaintance in an inn, like the unfortunate Wopsle, and even to the wine he drinks.

In his practice Jaggers adheres always to 'the strict line of fact'; he demands exact figures and forces those with whom he has to deal to make definite statements. He makes no admissions and, in fairness, warns others not to commit themselves. 'Take nothing on its looks; take everything on evidence', is his motto. He makes no recommendations and allows no questions (this is Wemmick's province). Until absolute proof is forthcoming or where the slightest caution is necessary, Jaggers prefers to treat the subject under discussion as purely hypothetical. He draws a significant distinction between Pip's being 'told' by Magwitch and his being 'informed'.

Pip never forgets the details of Jaggers's appearance at their first chance meeting on the stairs at Satis and he checks them off when he encounters him again at the village inn.

His large head, his dark complexion, his deep-set eyes, his bushy black eyebrows, his large watch-chain, his strong black dots of beard and whisker, and even the smell of scented soap on his great hand.

Jaggers regularly washes his hands and face after hours as if washing off his clients; and the halo of scented soap precedes him as he forces his way through the unfortunates hanging about his office door. The wall opposite his chair is greasemarked by the shoulders of those who endure his relentless questionings. The brass nails on his high-backed chair remind Pip of a coffin, as the loops of the carved garlands on the panelled walls of the lawyer's rooms remind him of the hangman's noose.

Jaggers never laughs and never relaxes, except once when he actually sighs when Wemmick ventures to suggest that he might be looking forward to a pleasant home in his retirement. Only once does he give a slight sign of being startled – when Pip tells him the identity of Estella's father. The inflexible manner, however, swiftly returns, a manner which, Wemmick explains, is purely professional and intended to puzzle. While awaiting an answer, Jaggers sways forward till his boots creak, or pauses with an enormous silk handkerchief – his chief weapon – in his hands halfway to his nose. This very gesture is often sufficient in itself to elicit the information he wants. When he grows impatient or utters a warning he frowns and bites his huge forefinger at his victim.

It is Jaggers' phrase that gives the book its title. He sees Pip making a wrong assumption and could put him right with a hint but this would mean violating his professional code of honour. He is not the least remarkable of Dickens's set of men of law.

Wemmick

'Here's Mr Pip, Aged Parent'

Unlike his chief, Wemmick leaves the office behind him when he goes home to the suburb of Walworth. Here he indulges his fancy as 'Jack-of-all-trades' with a variety of devices too numerous for a small wooden cottage and garden, were it not that everything is on a miniature scale. In the genial atmosphere of the 'Walworth sentiment' Pip feels at home as nowhere else since his departure from the forge; he certainly is given kindly advice which would never have been proffered in the office where business is conducted in a formal and even hostile spirit. Wemmick is seen at his best in his tender treatment of the Aged Parent who is regularly nodded at, patiently listened to while he reads from the newspaper and allowed to fire the gun and work the drawbridge.

No one has surpassed Dickens in the presentation of genuine home life; and the simplicity, regularity and wholesomeness of the 'Castle' is in strong contrast to the fantastic state of affairs at Hammersmith.

Wemmick's most pronounced feature is his 'post-office' slit of a mouth, set in a square, wooden face. His respect for his employer is considerable; he carries official precaution to an extreme, as when he requests the immediate burning of the letter warning Pip to get Magwitch away, an obscurely worded missive that could have given nobody away.

Even when Wemmick arranges his wedding, his secretive methods have the upper hand, and an innocent fishing expedition is turned, by a series of surprises, into a perfectly organized ceremony at a quiet country church. A last touch is his depositing of his white gloves in the font on leaving. Miss Skiffins, equally wooden in appearance, equally methodical in her ways and long accustomed to the routine at the 'Castle', though now a 'Walworth sentiment' on no account to be mentioned to Mr Jaggers, would undoubtedly, besides managing his fowls, effect such a change in Wemmick from his customary bachelor appearance as would hardly escape that vigilant eye. Then, it may be supposed, they would be on bad terms with one another until some unfortunate client offered himself for browbeating and enabled them to re-establish a good understanding on the old footing of professional inflexibility!

While Mr Jaggers maintained a judicial ignorance of the ex-convict's whereabouts Wemmick spares no pains to keep a close watch on developments. His motto is, 'Get hold of portable property', and his person is decked with mementoes of executed clients.

Herbert

'My poor dear Handel, I am too stunned to think'

If Pip is deprived of childhood companionship, he is blessed as a young man with a sympathetic and true friend. Herbert has been 'tried' by Miss Havisham, presumably for Estella to practise upon, but has failed, as he was likely to fail in his realization of 'Capital', had not Pip created a partnership for him. When first encountered pale, pimply and angular, and determined on sparring with Pip in the garden at Satis, Herbert takes the blows dealt him by Pip with the same airy inconsequence with which he later withstands the 'buffets of poverty' while 'looking about him' in London. Herbert's only qualification for success in life is a hopeful disposition. He is, however, a frank and easy companion and gives Pip sound advice and, though he expresses admiration of the latter's businesslike way of ticking off their debts and allowing a 'margin', Pip has to admit that, given his 'opening', Herbert is to prove the better businessman. He is fortunate too in the devotion of Clara Barley, a 'captive fairy' attendant on her 'ogre' of a father. When these two are married out in the East, 'Handel' is to find a third home with them.

Minor characters

The background of the story is well filled with lesser characters encountered by Pip. Some of these are given whole episodes to themselves with little bearing on the plot but providing interest as sketches or in some cases caricatures from real life; others appear once only and are not heard of again. However, with few exceptions and no matter how odd their idiosyncrasies, they convey the impression of being very much alive, an achievement in characterization which is Dickens's supreme gift as a novelist. For convenience they are here sketched in groups.

Pumblechook that 'liar and hypocrite' is foremost among the visitors at the forge. He has 'a mouth like a fish, dull staring eyes, and sandy hair standing upright on his head'. Little in fiction is more despicable than his claim to be Pip's benefactor: after heaping insults and arithmetical sums on the blacksmith's boy, Pumblechook goes out of his way to shake hands with the young man of fortune and even tries to wheedle him into investing money into his business. When Pumblechook is ignored, he fills the press and the neighbourhood with his lies; when Pip, his prospects ruined and his health impaired, stops at the Blue Boar on his way back to Joe, the old impostor delivers a pompous lecture to him on his ingratitude.

Mr Wopsle, the parish clerk with his Roman nose and deep, declamatory voice, reappears in London as a Shakespearian actor. Having failed in this role he is later seen in an amazing variety of stage parts. 'Mr Waldengarver' as Hamlet and later in pantomime is given the best part of two chapters (31 and 47) for his extraordinary performances, together with the reactions of his audience, not to mention his recitation of George Barnwell and his dramatic reading of the murder case in which he is so sharply pulled up by Mr Jaggers. His great-aunt's academy is the most farcical burlesque in the book.

Orlick is more sinister than Compeyson simply because we see more of his slouching figure, 'dancing' at Biddy, creeping up behind Mrs Joe to fell her with the cast-off leg-iron, or drunkenly preparing to kill Pip and burn his body in the limekiln. He ends up in gaol for the burglary of Pumblechook's shop. Nothing Orlick does, not even his spying or his melodramatic attempt on Pip's life, has any influence on the plot (Mrs Joe might have been made to die a natural death); the chief reason for his existence would seem to be to make the reader's flesh creep.

Sarah Pocket is equally sinister but quite harmless: in her wig and hideous muslin cap she keeps the door at Satis, growing ever more green and yellow at the thought of others benefiting from Miss Havisham's will and receiving in the end only twenty-five pounds a year for her services. The other toadies, Georgiana and Camilla, are similarly served.

In London, we are taken to the Hammersmith household once and no more.

Matthew Pocket, who so offended Miss Havisham by telling her the truth about Compeyson, manages by tutoring young gentle-men and doing some litrary hack-work to maintain a large family in a respectable riverside residence, staffed by a retinue of servants. Distracted by frequent domestic mishaps, he gives ludicrous expression to his helplessness and perplexity by trying to lift himself up by his hair and our last glimpse of him is in a state of collapse on the sofa after a particularly inane remark by his wife.

Mrs Pocket is one more example of the author's unsympathetic treatment of the upper-classes or those who lay claim to gentility of birth or breeding: Drummle is a boor, Compeyson a villain, Miss Havisham unbalanced, the Finches empty-headed and the Brandleys mere ciphers in the story. Daughter of a would-be baronet and mother of seven children 'tumbling up', Mrs Pocket spends hours poring over family pedigrees, oblivious of the things she leaves lying about. Her 'aristocratic disposition' being so accustomed to luxury and elegance, she might be ornamental but, as mistress of a household, completely useless. Like Miss Havisham she has an attendant toady in Mrs Coiler.

Bentley Drummle, the 'Spider' as Jaggers nicknames him, is really a well-bred Orlick, being two removes from a baronetcy; 'idle, proud, niggardly, reserved and suspicious', he is content to lie in wait for his opportunity. Drummle sneers at others for lending him money and toasts Estella with a leer at Pip. The ensuing challenge comes to nothing as Estella accepts his addresses and finally marries him, enduring many years of ill-treatment at his hands.

Startop, though spoilt as a boy, is an agreeable, forgiving young man, who assists Pip and Herbert on the day of the attempted escape abroad.

Clara Barley, a rather démure young lady, disliked her lover's 'expensive companion' on principle and Pip does not get to meet Herbert's betrothed for some time. He finds her to be gentle and confiding but subject to her tyrant father, a former ship's purser who, when not stamping on the floor for attention, doling out his 'stores' or sweeping the river with his telescope, lies on the bed muttering a blasphemous refrain about himself.

Themes

Few novelists have written books with such clarity of purpose behind them as Dickens. His attacks on social evils, such as the Poor Law in *Oliver Twist*, the Court of Chancery in *Bleak House*, imprisonment for debt in *David Copperfield* and the Yorkshire schools in *Nicholas Nickleby*, led in some cases to reforms. Whereas in earlier novels this moral purpose is apt to be obtruded on the reader, it is not so in *Great Expectations*. Here the story comes a long way first, and the lessons to be drawn from it are only to be inferred.

First of these is the influence of money on human character. It pervades the book. The Pockets (with the exception of Matthew and his family) greedily hope to benefit from Miss Havisham's will and that lady maliciously enjoys making them envious of Pip who in reality is not the favoured one. Pip himself, having seen his small earnings as a boy regularly confiscated, has his head turned by unexpected affluence and soon leads not only himself but Herbert into serious debt. A most demoralizing spectacle to Pip is the complete change of manner on the part of the tradesmen, Trabb and Pumblechook. That money can be put to good purpose is demonstrated by Miss Havisham's payment of Pip's apprenticeship fees; the buying of Herbert's partnership; and the bequest to Matthew that followed Pip's praise of him. Magwitch's use of his wealth was an act of devotion and Pip's decision to forego it, though at first made on snobbish grounds, is continued in a spirit of remorseful sacrifice.

Hardly less important is the hollowness of a false gentility. In this respect Pip is the example by which to take warning. A pretty girl, reared in better circumstances, first makes him painfully aware of his own coarseness and the humble condition in which he lives. For her sake he longs to become a 'gentleman' and when he is so fortunate as to be able to live like one, wearing the right clothes, behaving correctly at table and eventually escorting the pretty girl on a round of social activities, he shamefully neglects the honest blacksmith who is his truest friend. Indeed, Pip is extremely embarrassed by Joe's uncouth behaviour in the presence of people like Herbert and Miss Havisham.

It is difficult to estimate just how snobbish Pip is, since we are given only his own mental reactions; the bitter humiliation inflicted on him by Trabb's Boy may have been due to some conceit in his bearing or it may have been only a mischievous urchin's readiness to poke fun at the smartly dressed. What we do know is that, by the irony of fate, Pip rises above his station thanks to the whim of a convict of the coarsest type and that, when his career is wrecked, he is patiently nursed back to health by the awkward, inarticulate Joe whom he has avoided while he was a man of fashion. Both of these men have a pride of their own and they know their own shortcomings too well to attempt any kind of pretence. However, they have a depth of feeling that exceeds anything of which Pip seems capable; their affection for him surpasses in warmth and loyalty the romantic admiration Pip feels for Estella.

The character most worthy of admiration is, of course, Joe Gargery, and it is therefore quite probable that Dickens's positive purpose, as distinct from the negative ones just described – the deceptive lure of money and the fascination of a false gentility – was to show wherein true gentlemanliness lies. Lacking in birth and breeding, the village blacksmith is loyal, considerate, patient, tactful and forgiving, in contrast with his young apprentice who, though a boy of naturally kind instincts, is betrayed by his ambition to appear a gentleman into selfishness, meanness, moral cowardice and all the outward trappings of snobbery.

Setting

Period

Without suggesting that Dickens had any particular years in mind (the book is quite devoid of dates), we can place the events of the story fairly accurately by means of 'internal evidence'. Pip was twenty-three when he practised 'shooting' Old London Bridge which was demolished in 1831 after the opening of the new bridge; he was just under twenty-one when, escorting Estella one night, he came into the glare of gas, not used for street illumination before 1827. These two references would make the year of his birth approximately 1807, five years before that of his creator: in writing the novel, Dickens, as well as Pip, would be looking back on his youth.

Among other details may be noted Orlick's use of the old flint, steel and tinder-box, superseded in 1837 by matches (called 'lucifer matches' at the time); Pip's thought of adding a balloon to his fictious tale of wonders at Satis House (ballooning became very popular in the 1820s); the steam-traffic on the Thames (started in 1816) 'far below its present extent', and watermen's boats (later eliminated by land transport) 'far more numerous'. An interesting allusion is the comparison of Pip, in his fear of the theft of the pie being found out, moving the table to 'a medium of the present day'; as Spiritualism did not reach Britain till 1852, Pip must have been writing his memoirs at the age of at least forty-five.

There are a limited number of minor social features of the early nineteenth century, such as musical glasses, waxworks at fairs, tarwater and rushlights, but nothing of the economic distress and political upheavals of the time. The novel, beginning in the Napoleonic wars and ending in the years of Parliamentary reform, moves in a fantastic little world of its own, its only contact with outside affairs lying in the grim sphere of law-court and prison. Pip's upbringing was to be associated with crime and no other factors must be allowed to interfere with this conception.

Of crime and its detection and punishment we are given vividly realistic pictures. Robberies were common, sentences ferocious and prisons horrible institutions. At the beginning of the century the penalty for over 150 offences was death by hanging, which was a public spectacle. The last public hanging in Britain was not until 1868. Magwitch was condemned with thirty-one others; these others would meet their fates early in the morning and be cut down before nine o'clock. On the marshes stood one of those gibbets on which malefactors were left hanging, and condemned men were to be encountered, manacled and fettered, among one's fellow-travellers on public coaches. Until the establishment of a regular police force in 1829, police work was mainly done by soldiers, while special investigations were entrusted to those 'extinct red-waist-coated police', the Bow Street runners, satirized by Dickens (as their successors have been in modern detective fiction) for absurd blunders like suspecting Joe of the murder of his wife!

Topography

In his last novels Dickens returned to his own district, the neighbourhood of Rochester and, though no names in this Kentish region are given (in contrast with London which is mapped out in detail) there is no doubt about the localities concerned.

The marshes

In the tongue of land lying between the estuaries of the Thames and the Medway, the Cooling and Cliffe Marshes stretch from the villages of the same names northwards to the bank of the Thames. Their flatness and 'bleak stillness' throw into relief the beacon (the Shorne Mead Light) and the old Battery (probably Shorne Mead). About two miles downriver would be the cement works near which Pip is nearly murdered. Round Lower Hope Point a path skirts the edge of the Thames leading to the landing stage where the convicts were taken back to the Hulks. For a long time after Pip's day seven old Hulks were moored off-shore and used as powder magazines. The marshes were crossed by sluices, each with its miniature windmill and muddy sluice-gate; there were reeds and rushes in the swampy parts, while cattle were pastured on the expanse of grass.

The village

Some five miles north of Rochester is the lonely churchyard of Cooling, and among its quaint gravestones can be seen the lozenges so humorously treated in the first page of the book. In Pip's time it was overgrown with nettles and brambles; the tower had a steeple and weathercock; between it and the sea was the horizontal line of marshes, across which would sweep the wild sea wind. About one mile from the marshes was the forge, with the wooden cottage of the blacksmith. Nearby was the 'Three Jolly Bargemen' and at the end of the lane the signpost, at one time a ghostly finger hovering in the mist, at another the last link with home.

The town

Only in Chapter 49 does Pip refer to the cathedral tower and the sound of its bells, thus identifying the town as the city of Rochester. The 'Blue Boar' has been located in the 'Bull Hotel' where Mr Pickwick and his friends stayed. Among the great man's notes on this occasion is a comment on soldiers staggering about under the influence of too much drink: 'the following them about, and jesting with them, affords a cheap and innocent amusement for the boy population.' Satis House was 'Restoration House' in the Vines (originally the Monks' Vineyard). However, the name was taken from another mansion, close to the Castle and so-called because, when Queen Elizabeth was asked by her host, after he had entertained her there for one night whether her accommodation had been satisfactory, she is said to have replied, "Satis"! In chapter 29 Pip describes the exterior of the house with its 'seared red brick walls, blocked windows, and strong green ivy clasping even the stacks of the chimneys with its twigs and tendons.' Outside is a wilderness of a garden and a disused brewery, strewn with empty casks; inside, a succession of dark passages, leading to the two rooms where, lit by candles in sconces high up on the walls, the half-mad, witchlike Miss Havisham, surrounded by the decaying remnants of the wedding-feast, torments her relatives, gloats over Estella's beauty and feeds herself with scraps at midnight.

In the High Street of the 'quiet old town' stands not only Pumblechook's corn-and-seed shop and Trabb's, the tailor's, but the premises of numerous tradesmen among whom business is so sluggish that they spend much of their time watching each other.

The capital

The journey to London by stage-coach took five hours, the terminus being the Cross Keys in Wood Street, Cheapside. Pip is awed by the capital's immensity but disgusted by its ugliness and dirt. After a short acquaintance with the filth of Smithfield and the grimness of Newgate Prison, where he is shown the gallows and whipping-post, Pip finds himself billeted in Barnard's Inn, 'the dingiest collection of shabby buildings ever squeezed together in a rank corner as a club for Tom-cats' and concludes that London is 'decidedly over-rated'.

Pip is destined to see more of Newgate. His tour of the cells with Wemmick is described in Chapter 32. The trial scene, in which the thirty-two capital sentences are pronounced together, is given in Chapter 56. In 1864, shortly before these executions ceased to be public spectacles, a crowd of fifty thousand saw a murderer hanged, barrels of beer being provided for the occasion. The gallows stood very close to the present entrance to the Central Criminal Court in Old Bailey.

The Temple, to which Pip and Herbert migrate from Barnard's Inn, was then rather lonely and exposed to the wind off the river. Hammersmith, where the eccentric Pockets live, and Richmond, the home of the aristocratic Brandleys, were then separated from London by miles of country road. South of the Thames was the suburb of Walworth and the 'Castle' of Wemmick. Jaggers lives in Gerrard Street, Soho. Apart from Herbert's humble place of employment, very little is seen of the background of teeming city life by which Pip is surrounded for some four years – lamplighters, a chop-house, a lodging-house and the theatre.

The river

As the ebb tide flowed past the Temple, Herbert thinks of it as carrying everything to his beloved Clara at Chinks's Basin; Pip dreads to think that somewhere on its surface Magwitch's pursuers are hastening to arrest him. Pip's journeys by river afford little glimpses of the great waterway down which Magwitch was transported to Australia to return years later, wealthy but still a convict; the river on which, not only changed in heart himself but having wrought a change of heart in the boy he had made into a gentleman, he meets his fate.

On that last ill-starred expedition the three young men cast off from Temple Stairs, thread their way through a maze of small craft, passing Old London Bridge, Billingsgate with its oyster-boats and Dutch vessels and the Tower with its Traitor's

Gate, observe the outward-bound steamers and reach Mill Pond Stairs. As the drama approaches its climax and the anxious crew of the rowing-boat scan the shipping and the shores for signs of danger, the descriptive part of the narrative becomes more detailed: cables and hawsers, buoys and ships' figureheads, scum and flotsam, the mingled noises of hammers, sawmills, pumps, capstans and shouting. After Gravesend they pass the floating Custom House, emigrant ships and troop transports and come to the marshy stretches where decrepit landing-stages, dilapidated light houses and rows of stakes stick up out of the mud and slime. Stealing past mysterious creeks, they put up at a dirty, suspicious-looking tavern, where the serving man gets his clothes from the bodies of the drowned.

The scenes amidst which Pip waits for his expectations to be realized are uniformly depressing, brightened, however, by the cheerful personalities of Herbert Pocket and Wemmick. On the other hand, those social occasions at which Pip has been destined by his unknown benefactor to play a conspicuous part are blighted by the disagreeable Drummle and the tantalizing relationship with Estella.

Atmosphere

After a series of rather gloomy novels (*Bleak House, Hard Times* and *Little Dorrit*) Dickens recovered some of his earlier high spirits and playful humour in *Great Expectations*. Though, as we have seen, there is still plenty of bleakness and hardness, the reader is once more regularly amused by the irresistibly comic writing; and deeply moved by two of the author's greatest creations from humble life: Joe Gargery and Abel Magwitch. There is, too, an underlying vein of gently cynical fun, possibly at the expense of himself: in the 'Castle' where the drawbridge and bower may be a tilt at his own 'vanities' at Gad's Hill Place, with its underground passage to the Swiss chalet in 'The Wilderness' on the other side of the road; in Pip's array of books, from which he read to Magwitch 'foreign languages wot I don't understand'; in Wopsle's love of recitation which led him to a stage career in which he played many parts.

There is considerable play of light and shadow symbolizing the bright prospects and the hidden scheming that shape the story. Predominant are the mists of the marshes, in the half-lights of which familiar objects loom up like phantoms; when the mists rise to give way to sunlight, they seem to reveal to Pip what life offers him; on his first journey to London, the world lies spread before him; on his return from his sister's funeral, the plain truth that years are to pass before he visits his old home again; at his final meeting with Estella, the knowledge that he will never be parted from her again. More frequent than the sunshine in which Pip talks with Biddy or Herbert is the presence of artificial light: the candles in Satis, the new gas-lamps in the London streets lit at dusk by an army of lamp-lighters, the old-fashioned rushlight in the Hummums, the reading-lamp with which Pip first receives 'Provis', the candle held up by Orlick while he gloats over his helpless 'enemy'.

The use of sounds is also effective, particularly the slight noises heard in an oppressive stillness: the rasping of a file in the eerie quiet of the marshes, the mice behind the panels of Satis, the nocturnal creakings in the Hummums, the mysterious ripples as the fugitives creep down river in the dark.

Death figures prominently in Dickens's novels and few of its aspects are missing from this book, from the gravestones with whose help Pip started learning his letters to the deathbed of Magwitch. There is also the shock of his sister's death, followed by the farcical spectacle of the funeral in full mourning; Miss Havisham's death from injuries by fire and her former lover's death by drowning; Pip's vivid recollections of his past life as he watches his would-be murderer's movements; and in the background the shadow of the gallows which the ex-convict cheated in the end.

Home life is equally prominent. There are two real homes: firstly, the forge, after Mrs Gargery's bitter tongue has been put to silence. From it Pip is separated by the influence of money and the attraction of Estella, but it retains its hold on his affections for, before leaving for the East, he has to say goodbye to his old bedroom under the roof and to the signpost at the end of the lane. It has been 'sanctified' for him by Joe's character. And secondly, the 'Castle', on which its owner lavishes his ingenuity. Here the 'Walworth sentiment' creates an atmosphere far removed from that of Jaggers's office and finds its supreme expression in Wemmick's tender and patient care of the Aged Parent.

The cloak of secrecy casts its folds over many parts. Pip himself is a repository of secrets, from the opening chapter when he becomes the unwilling accomplice of a runaway convict to the tracking down of Estella's parentage. His own career is a secret and in secret he starts Herbert on his career. Infinite precautions are taken in Jaggers's office to prevent secrets from leaking out, and the habit is comically maintained by Wemmick at his marriage, the wedding ceremony being disguised as a fishing expedition. Equally great precautions are taken by Pip and Herbert in their attempt to prevent Magwitch's arrest; the movements which lead to his recognition and tracking down are wrapped in mystery.

Dickens's novels are full of people with expectations (of whom Micawber in *David Copperfield* is the best-known example) and in them there is frequent expectation of good and frequent dread of evil. Most of Pip's time is spent in expectation of realizing his fortune or in dread of exposure; Herbert 'looked about him' for an opportunity of making 'Capital'; the Pockets (except those at Hammersmith) toady to Miss Havisham in expectation of benefiting from her will; that lady herself lives for the day when Estella will work out her scheme of revenge on the male sex.

Events in fiction as well as in life turn out differently from what is anticipated and come often as surprises when least expected. Pip longs to be a gentleman and fit for Estella's company when suddenly he is spirited into fashionable life only to find a gulf between him and the object of his devotion; when Magwitch climbs the stairs with his bulging pocketbook, Pip prefers poverty to his fortune; Herbert's opportunity is found for him by his friend; the Pockets, jealous of the wrong person, find themselves passed over in favour of the one member of their family who has not toadied; Miss Havisham suffers agonies of remorse at the moment of her triumph.

Dickens was apt to stretch coincidence to the limit of the incredible: that Miss Havisham and Magwitch should employ the same lawyer is just plausible, but Pip's meeting with Estella in the ruins of Satis reads too much like a fairy tale.

Structure

In this novel Dickens returned to the autobiographical method of *David Copperfield*; like his better-known prototype Pip recounts the cruel circumstances of his boyhood and his heart-searching as a young man. The book has been called a 'novel without a hero' but this is hardly true in the literary sense, as Pip is the central character in all the major incidents, and rather unfair in the moral sense since, while he plays mainly a passive part waiting on events to shape his career, he is not devoid of noble instincts and generous resolves.

The fantastic story of Miss Havisham is framed in the far more convincing setting of the village on the edge of the marshes. The story begins and ends at the blacksmith's forge for Pip's reunion with Estella is no more than an epilogue. The contrast between the occupants of the big brick mansion and those of the humble wooden cottage is the starting point of Pip's false pilgrimage after gentility; when he returns years later, only the site of Satis House remains, but a happy little family is growing up at the smithy.

Pip is not only disappointed but deceived. His destiny was decided for him not by an eccentric patroness but by a transported convict toiling in the lonely sheep pastures of New South Wales. The taint of prison and crime which clung to him after that first encounter in the churchyard, and from which he sought to escape as from the 'commonness' of his upbringing, return with overwhelming force to shatter his dreams.

The whole development, in fact, is based on the opening chapters: the memory of Pip leads to Magwitch's reformation and his determination later to make the boy's fortune. The ex-convict is not to know that his desire to remain anonymous until he can see his 'gentleman' for himself leads Pip into believing that he is being made fit by Miss Havisham to marry Estella, a belief to which the young man clings even while he knows that Estella has been trained to victimize those who fall in love with her. Thus we have the curious position that while the beauty of Magwitch's daughter is being used by Miss Havisham to break Pip's heart, the wealth of the father is being lavished on him because he has reminded the tough old gaol-bird of the very same daughter; further, Pip shrinks from Magwitch because of the beauty and breeding he associates with Magwitch's daughter! The reader can hardly ask for anything more involved. Estella, whom Pip loved first and last, is the instrument on the one hand of grotesque spite towards him and, on the other, of grotesque generosity.

In these days it is difficult to think in terms of monthly magazine parts but that was the way in which the majority of Dickens's novels appeared. It was a method which imposed a strain on the author, especially one so devoted to the interests of his reading public as Dickens, and the results are often to be seen in hasty composition, unreal incidents, superfluous characters and lapses in style. It seems sometimes as if Dickens feels bound to provide both humour and pathos in a single instalment. That alternation is noticeable in *Great Expectations*: the farcical encounter with Drummle comes between Magwitch's life history and Pip's declaration of love to Estella; Wemmick's wedding between the arrest of Magwitch and his trial. Pip's escape from the clutches of Orlick is a piece of unnecessary melodrama, calculated perhaps to relieve the tension of waiting for the moment of getting 'Provis' on board an outward-bound steamer.

The book is divided into three 'stages': the first, Chapters 1–19, ends with Pip's departure for London to be educated as a gentleman; the second, Chapters 20–39, ends with the appearance of his real benefactor; the third, Chapters 40–58, ends with Pip's departure for the East; and the final chapter effects a change in the ending that had been suggested by Dickens's friend, Bulwer Lytton. 'I have no doubt,' the author wrote, 'the story will be the more acceptable through the alteration.'

This was certainly a concession to the feelings of his readers; it would have been an artistic ending for Pip to lose Estella but it would have been very unpopular. As it is, it is a sad little reunion and vaguely inconclusive. The film version of the novel made quite certain of the matter by bringing them together immediately after Pip's recovery and sparing them eleven years of separation. The title logically suggests 'Great Disappointments' but our sympathy with the blacksmith's boy, whose life, moral as well as material, has been moulded by his expectations, requires an ending which satisfies our emotion rather than our reason.

There is, too, enough of tragedy in the fate of Magwitch. The old man dies happy in the thought of his boy enjoying his wealth and loving his daughter; it would have been too much for the reader that both of these beliefs should be illusions. The scenes in which Magwitch is concerned are the most vivid in the book and Dickens was at his best in working up to a climax like the final capture of the ex-convict.

The period between the announcement of Pip's expectations and their collapse is filled by Dickens with an array of characters and a succession of scenes in which his creative fancy had full play. The opening and closing chapters are, on the other hand, intensely dramatic. A noteworthy feature is the way in which the chief villain of the book is seen only by glimpses, crouching in a ditch, in a theatre audience or in a boat; we see the results of his scheming, but he works out of sight most of the time. The manner of his death is a well-deserved punishment for the misery he had brought upon others.

Style

The chief characteristics of Dickens's prose are its simplicity, its emotional quality and its frequent use of humorous turns of phrase. He wrote with huge enjoyment, if sometimes under considerable strain. In a jovial mood he would exaggerate to the limit; in sad moments he could achieve the tenderest pathos with the simplest expression. His material did not call for the subtle arts of the fine writer; at his best he used pure English in vigorous and racy narrative and perfect clarity of sentence structure. There are, however, occasions, only too often, when he descended to unbelievable bathos, cheap jokes and maudlin sentiment.

Dickens's literary training was imperfect – in fact he owed more to his journalistic experience than to other authors, of whom Fielding and Smollett influenced him most – but he strove hard to improve his style. Largely self-educated, he had faults and mannerisms that offend the purist; nevertheless, they are swallowed up in the zest with which he arrests the reader's attention and in the wealth of detail and colour with which he invests his characters and incidents. He started his regular public readings in 1853, and his later novels, including *Great Expectations*, may well have been written in places with an eye on future declamation. The book is certainly sprinkled with passages that would recite well and with character sketches that lend themselves to humorous impersonation.

As if to counterbalance the grim circumstances and dismal atmosphere of much of the story, humorous treatment is much more frequent than pathos: Pip and Herbert making memoranda of their debts, Wopsle's stage performances and Wemmick's wedding provide comic interludes. Frequently these incidents are strained to the limits of the farcical: the Pocket baby and the nutcrackers; Pumblechook shaking hands; Trabb's Boy mocking Pip; Wemmick's courting; Drummle's driving; and the funeral procession. The description of Jaggers in court; 'Mr Waldengarver' as Hamlet; and the waiter providing 'tea' for Pip and Estella, are typical examples of Dickens's humour. Joe writing a letter is strongly reminiscent of Sam Weller in *Pickwick Papers*.

There is pathos in Pip's departures from home and in the death of Magwitch. Pip whose tears soon dry after the signpost has been left behind; or when Joe, forgotten in thoughts of Estella, is the cause of tears shed by others; Joe when parting with him, Miss Havisham when asking his forgiveness, Estella when recollecting many years later how she had first rejected his love, Magwitch at his first cold welcome.

There are occasional satirical touches: Mr Pocket's lectures on domestic economy; Mrs Pocket's father being knighted for composing the address at the laying of a foundation stone by Royalty; the greasy condition of a fashionable eating-house; the gentility of brewing as compared with baking; the police suspecting Joe of the assault on his wife; the dark state of his wife's mind after the attack, in finding no more meaning in the simplest words than in an election cry!

Dickens excels in the apt phrase: the windows in Barnard's Inn consisting of 'dilapidated blind and curtain, crippled flower-pot, cracked glass, dusty decay, and miserable makeshift'; the candles at Satis that 'faintly troubled its darkness'; Matthew Pocket wondering vaguely why his children had not been 'billeted by Nature on somebody else'. Simile is frequently used to portray some aspect of a character's appearance: the newly wed Mrs Wemmick being embraced like a cello; Orlick like a human doormouse in the porter's room at Satis; Joe and Pip crossing their fingers like the legs of Crusaders' effigies (probably seen by Pip in the Temple Church); Joe in his Sunday clothes like a 'scarecrow in good circumstances'; the boy Pip being goaded by the grown-ups 'like an unfortunate little bull in a Spanish arena'.

Some of these expressions are passed off as Pip's 'homely thoughts', like the neglected box-tree resembling a pudding that has stuck to the saucepan and got burnt. A certain amount of artificial liveliness is obtained by the personification of inanimate objects: the houses peeping in through Jaggers's skylight; the flower-seeds pining in Pumblechook's packets as if in gaol; the bellows in Joe's forge roaring after the runaway convicts. To Pip's imaginative mind animal life assumes human attitudes; the once accusing cattle show a new respect for a young man of fortune; the rooks warn him of Estella's departure from Satis; and in the old house are the agitated spiders and aldermanic beetles.

There are several passages of sordidly realistic detail; the manacled convicts with their flavour of 'bread-poultice, baize, rope-yarn and hearth-stone'; the depressing hotel room in which Pip and Estella have tea; the infested lodging-house where Pip spends the night away from his rooms; the river surface on the way to Gravesend. Occasionally the smallest details, particularly of furnishing, are obtruded on our notice, as if there could not be enough true-to-life background: the china poodles on Mrs Joe's parlour mantelshelf; the umbrella over the 'Stinger'; the formally clipped trees at Richmond; the gravy stains on tavern tablecloths.

There are numerous examples of Dickens's mannerisms. Humorous periphrasis, the most characteristic of them all, is scattered throughout the book: 'Long after these constitutional powers had dispersed' for the departure of the constables from the forge; 'those obscure corners of pork of which the pig, when living, had had the least reason to be vain' for the scraps given to Pip; Mr Wopsle's great-aunt's pupils emerging after school uttering 'shrieks of intellectual victory'. This habit may have derived from the author's early experience of newspapers – a typical specimen of journalese' is Pumblechook's 'puff' in Chapter 28.

Sometimes this roundabout way of saying things is overdone, as in 'conquered a confirmed habit of living' for 'died'; perhaps Wemmick's caution may excuse such a roundabout expression as 'a certain part of the world where a good many people go, not always in gratification of their own inclinations, and not quite irrespective of the government', yet there seems no good reason why, in private conversation he should not have said 'Australia', unless it be Dickens's own 'confirmed habit' of long-winded allusions! A similar and quite effective trick is the accumulation of synonyms: 'The bill paid, and the waiter remembered, and the ostler not forgotten, and the chambermaid taken into consideration – in a word, the whole house bribed into a state of contempt and animosity, and Estella's purse much lightened.' Critical comment, worthy of a modern purist, is expended on Orlick's use of 'jiggered' in Chapter 17 and in Joe's phrase, 'a *cool* four thousand' in Chapter 57.

Other kinds of emphasis are seen in simple repetition: 'mud, mud, mud, deep in all the streets'; 'I could never, never, never, undo what I had done.' And groups of four closely associated words: Pip found London 'ugly, crooked, narrow and dirty' and the interior of Newgate 'frozy, ugly, disorderly and depressing'; he turned with disgust from Smithfield 'asmear with filth and fat and blood and foam.' When he first saw Magwitch, the convict 'limped and shivered, and glared and growled'; another convict summed up life in the Hulks as 'mudbank, mist, swamp and work: work, swamp, mist and mudbank'. There are even larger groups of words – Mrs Joe's merciless washing of Pip: 'I was soaped and kneaded, and towelled, and thumped, and harrowed, and rasped'; Wopsle's idea of educating Pip by declaiming dramatic passages at him, with appropriate gestures, so that Pip was 'contradicted and embraced and wept over and bullied and clutched and stabbed and knocked about in a variety of ways'. And, of course, there is exaggeration: Pip seeing 'miles of open country' through Mr Hubble's legs, or the shopkeepers in town engaged in watching each other, like links in a chain.

Dickens is sometimes guilty of a clumsy conceit: the smells in Barnard's Inn suggesting to Pip that he should 'Try Barnard's Mixture'; those who rumpled Pip's hair described as taking 'ophthalmic steps' to patronize him; and the extraordinary confirmation that Wopsle had sat down several times in the wet by the removal of his coat – whereupon 'the circumstantial evidence on his trousers would have hanged him if it had been a capital offence'. Pip's confused state of mind may possibly excuse a mixed metaphor, when he described Trabb's Boy as 'an invulnerable and dodging serpent who, when chased into a corner, flew out again between his captor's legs, scornfully yelping'. Dickens's faults, however, have been truly described as 'the excess of his virtues' and we overlook gross exaggeration under the stimulus of his vigorous narrative powers.

Apart from Wopsle's recitations there are no literary allusions. An eastern fable provides an elaborate analogy at the end of Chapter 38 for the blow about to befall Pip, though the parallel to the Sultan's cutting of the fatal rope is not clear.

One final note. The trial scene in Chapter 56 (five paragraphs) shows Dickens at his best: the scene is concisely but colourfully portrayed, vivid in its contrasts; with implied condemnation of an inhuman system and shrewd glances at human failings, dignity and depravity. And there is detailed realism; and symbolism, as in the sunbeam linking Life and Eternity.

General questions plus questions on related topics for coursework/examinations on other books you may be studying

1 To what extent should this novel be regarded as a social study? Has it a moral lesson?

Suggested notes for essay answer:

In his earlier novels Dickens openly attacked social evils as embodied in institutions whose low standards, however, were largely due to human defects of character, such as dishonesty or brutality. In this later one the reader is shown – the effect of money on a particular personality in unusual circumstances – young man who has been persecuted at home and deprived of real enjoyment since childhood: made conscious of his lowly status and his lack of breeding: suddenly endowed with a handsome income from a mysterious source; closely connected with this advancement in society – romantic and lasting love for a girl of unusual personal beauty.

Pip, sensitive to insults, but also keenly aware of his own hurtful attitudes to others; ambitious less for his own satisfaction than to be a fitting partner for his beloved; ashamed to be associated with the uncouth appearance and behaviour of the two men to whom ultimately he realizes he owes most. This selfish reaction is feelingly understood and allowed for by both blacksmith and convict; each has in different ways been devoted to him ever since he was a seven-year-old. Pip therefore not a 'type' – his career has been most inappropriately referred to as a 'snob's progress'. Other main characters not types; indeed they are individuals to a ridiculous and even grotesque degree. They seem specially chosen to figure in this fantastic plot – interwoven by two such eccentrics as a jilted bride living in immobilized seclusion and plotting a spiteful revenge, and a jail-bird accumulating a fortune by years of hard self-sacrifice to reward a boy who stole a pie for him in a crisis.

No serious study of social and economic life would run to such extremes: the brother of an atrociously oppressive elder sister becomes the constant companion for a time of a beautiful but strangely heartless woman; the penniless apprentice, whose services to Miss Havisham go unpaid except for the apprenticeship fee, is unexpectedly given the means to live in some style. The reality is that the beauty and the money derive from a social outcast; one is rediscovered after a lapse of years, the other lost by confiscation.

In Dickens's novels social problems essentially individual affairs, not national situations urgently requiring political solutions. His primary concern may well have been with entertaining his readers – the average reader is attracted more by personal dilemmas than moral judgments. Moral lessons are guides to future behaviour: in *Great Expectations* forgiveness comes, as often, too late, after all the harm has been done. The evil motive which precipitated the action of the novel can be imputed to greed for money (Arthur's jealousy of his half-sister's inheritance) but this is too familiar a vice to be a social 'problem'. The title 'Great Expectations' implies ultimate disappointment – for Pip.

What moral lesson is to be drawn from the experiences of the main character? He has been criticized for his too passive reactions to misfortune or injustice, as well as his drift into snobbish attitudes. It is in character that the novel ends so inconclusively.

In his very individual case we can see spiritual realization overcoming material disappointment. When faith has been shaken and hopes wrecked, only love is left, to cast a mellowing gleam over the ruins laid bare when the mist has lifted.

2 How many kinds of expectations besides Pip's can you find, and how far was each realized?

3 On how many occasions is somebody taken by surprise? Give an account of one of these occasions.

4 Do you think the end appropriate and convincing?

5 Comment on three of the letters in the story and the purposes with which they are written.

6 What precautions are taken to keep 'Provis' safe from arrest in London?

7 Using material taken from the novel give an account of the criminal law proceedings of that time.

8 What contemporary pictures are given of (a) a funeral, (b) a visit to the theatre, (c) a dame's school, (d) a meal at an inn?

9 Describe Pip as seen by (a) Biddy, (b) Jaggers.

10 Contrast the escaped convict with the returned transport.

11 Illustrate (a) Rumblechook's hypocrisy, (b) Wemmick's caution, (c) Wopsle's acting.

12 Which characters get (a) most enjoyment, (b) least enjoyment out of life?

13 How many characters receive (a) the reward, (b) the punishment they deserve?

14 Which characters show (a) greed for money, (b) indifference to it?

15 In which characters do you find it hardest to believe?

16 What glimpses of the Thames are offered in different parts of the story?

17 Which passages, one in each case, do you find (a) most dramatic, (b) most humorous, (c) most pathetic?

18 Who were: Mr Waldengarver, Camilla, Mr Campbell, the Colonel, Arthur, Clarriker, Flopson, Mrs Coiler, the Spider, the young Telemachus?

19 What incidents are connected with the following places: the Temple, Little Britain, Chinks's Basin, Camberwell Green, the 'Blue Boar', the 'Three Jolly Bargemen'?

20 How many other titles can you think of for this novel? Justify your choice of one of these.

21 Write an account of any book you have read which is written as if it were autobiography.

22 Describe an escape or escapes in a book of your choice.

23 Show how a secret or secrets are revealed in a particular book. What effect does this have on the plot?

24 Write about any two characters in a book you have studied who are unusual in appearance and/or character.

25 Describe two incidents in any book which are noteworthy for their sense of fun, or which appeal to your sense of humour in some way.

26 Bring out clearly the exciting or dramatic qualities in any story you have read or in any play you have seen.

27 Write about the presentation of any character in a book you have studied who has been deeply changed by an event or events in the past.

28 Write about a character in one of your books whom you consider to be evil and who has few, if any, redeeming features.

29 Describe the presentation of ambition *or* snobbery *or* class differences in a book you know well.

30 Compare any character in *Great Expectations* with a character in a story or play you have read.

Further reading

The Life of Charles Dickens, John Forster (Dent, 1970)

Charles Dickens, K. J. Fielding (Longmans: Harmondsworth, (1965) Writers and their work series)

A Reader's Guide to Charles Dickens, P. Hobsbaum (Thames & Hudson: London, 1973)

The Dickens Theatre, R. Garis (Oxford University Press: Oxford)

The Dickens Encyclopedia, ed. Hayward (Routledge: London)

Charles Dickens: His Tragedy and Triumph, Edgar Johnson (Penguin: Harmondsworth, 1986)

Brodie's Notes

D. H. Lawrence	**The Rainbow**
D. H. Lawrence	**Sons and Lovers**
D. H. Lawrence	**Women in Love**
Harper Lee	**To Kill a Mockingbird**
Laurie Lee	**Cider with Rosie**
Christopher Marlowe	**Dr Faustus**
Arthur Miller	**The Crucible**
Arthur Miller	**Death of a Salesman**
John Milton	**Paradise Lost**
Robert C. O'Brien	**Z for Zachariah**
Sean O'Casey	**Juno and the Paycock**
George Orwell	**Animal Farm**
George Orwell	**1984**
J. B. Priestley	**An Inspector Calls**
J. D. Salinger	**The Catcher in the Rye**
William Shakespeare	**Antony and Cleopatra**
William Shakespeare	**As You Like It**
William Shakespeare	**Hamlet**
William Shakespeare	**Henry IV Part I**
William Shakespeare	**Julius Caesar**
William Shakespeare	**King Lear**
William Shakespeare	**Macbeth**
William Shakespeare	**Measure for Measure**
William Shakespeare	**The Merchant of Venice**
William Shakespeare	**A Midsummer Night's Dream**
William Shakespeare	**Much Ado about Nothing**
William Shakespeare	**Othello**
William Shakespeare	**Richard II**
William Shakespeare	**Romeo and Juliet**
William Shakespeare	**The Tempest**
William Shakespeare	**Twelfth Night**
George Bernard Shaw	**Pygmalion**
Alan Sillitoe	**Selected Fiction**
John Steinbeck	**Of Mice and Men** and **The Pearl**
Jonathan Swift	**Gulliver's Travels**
Dylan Thomas	**Under Milk Wood**
Alice Walker	**The Color Purple**
W. B. Yeats	**Selected Poetry**

ENGLISH COURSEWORK BOOKS

Terri Apter	**Women and Society**
Kevin Dowling	**Drama and Poetry**
Philip Gooden	**Conflict**
Philip Gooden	**Science Fiction**
Margaret K. Gray	**Modern Drama**
Graham Handley	**Modern Poetry**
Graham Handley	**Prose**
Graham Handley	**Childhood and Adolescence**
R. J. Sims	**The Short Story**